E-CRIT:
DIGITAL MEDIA, CRITICAL THEORY, AND THE HUMANITIES

In *E-Crit*, Marcel O'Gorman takes an ambitious and provocative look at how university scholarship, pedagogy, and curricula might be transformed to suit a digital culture. Arguing that universities were founded on the logic of print culture, O'Gorman sets out to reinvent the academic apparatus, constructing a hybrid methodology that draws on avant-garde art, deconstructive theory, cognitive science, and the work of painter and poet William Blake.

O'Gorman explores the ways in which digital media might help to restore the critical, intellectual purpose of higher education, which has been repressed by the technocratic structures that dominate the modern university. He argues that the revolutionary, socio-critical impetus that spurred deconstructive theory and transformed the humanities was lost in the initial attempts to digitize the literary canon and demonstrate the convergence of critical theory and hypertext. Humanities disciplines, he suggests, must reposition themselves through the invention of humanities-based interdisciplinary programs capable of adapting to the post-print vicissitudes of a digital culture. *E-Crit* is thus essential reading for anyone concerned with the practice – and future – of the humanities in higher education.

MARCEL O'GORMAN is an associate professor in the Department of English at the University of Waterloo.

E-CRIT

Digital Media, Critical Theory, and the Humanities

Marcel O'Gorman

UNIVERSITY OF TORONTO PRESS
Toronto Buffalo London

© University of Toronto Press Incorporated 2006
Toronto Buffalo London
Printed in Canada

Reprinted in paperback 2007

ISBN 978-0-8020-9037-9 (cloth)
ISBN 978-0-8020-9544-2 (paper)

Printed on acid-free paper

Library and Archives Canada Cataloguing in Publication

O'Gorman, Marcel
    E-crit : digital media, critical theory and the humanities / Marcel
    O'Gorman.

    Includes bibliographical references and index.
    ISBN 978-0-8020-9037-9 (bound). – ISBN 978-0-8020-9544-2 (pbk.)

    1. Humanities – Study and teaching (Higher) – Data processing.
    2. Humanities – Data processing.   3. Humanities – Research.   I. Title.

    PN98.E4O36 2006   001.3'0285   C2005-905500-6

This project was partially supported by funding from the Mellon Funds for
Humanistic Studies, University of Detroit Mercy.

University of Toronto Press acknowledges the financial assistance to its
publishing program of the Canada Council for the Arts and the Ontario Arts
Council.

University of Toronto Press acknowledges the financial support for its publishing
activities of the Government of Canada through the Book Publishing Industry
Development Program (BPIDP).

To Joyce and Bernard, for having eight.

Contents

LIST OF ILLUSTRATIONS

ACKNOWLEDGMENTS

There is a complex network of discourses running through the node of *E-Crit*. This makes it difficult for me to do justice to all its contributors. What I might offer instead is a series of provisional, though not purely fictitious, origins.

The project started, perhaps, in 1993, when Kevin O'Connor showed me how to cut and paste chunks of critical theory into Lotus Freelance Graphics. Or perhaps it started with the meeting of the two Steves: Steve Karamatos, who taught me the <img> tag in HTML, and Steve Gibb, whose grotesque paintings provided me with a mnemonic study guide in critical theory. Then again, it may have started when Hugh Culik and Nick Rombes, to whom I am deeply indebted, came up with the wild idea of launching something called an Electronic Critique Program at the University of Detroit Mercy, and asked me to direct it.

It is most likely, however, that the book began somewhere between my reading of *Teletheory* and *Heuretics*. These baffling texts inspired me to move from Windsor, Ontario, to Gainesville, Florida, so that I could work with Greg Ulmer and the Florida Research Ensemble. I am infinitely grateful to Greg for making theory accessible and exciting, and thankful to my 'Florida School' colleagues, including Robert Ray, who put up with a great deal of excitement and inaccessible prose when I tried to link William Blake, Walter Benjamin, and Roland Barthes by plotting their work on a graphic of the letter 'B.'

The first draft of the manuscript was written, out of sheer anxiety, in a nine-month race with my gestating daughter, Sophia. The race was then stretched out for a few more years at the University of Detroit Mercy, where members of the English Department 'tea party' patiently read chapters and encouraged me to find a publisher. The race may have gone on forever were it not for my wife, Beth, who is always quick to point out when I have been running too long.

Introduction

The only way open to eliminate the 'fascism in our heads' is to explore and build upon the open qualities of human discourse, and thereby to intervene in the way knowledge is produced and constituted at the particular sites where a localized power-discourse prevails.

— David Harvey, *The Condition of Postmodernity*, 45

New Media Calls for New Majors

On 19 December 2002 the 'Technology'-page headline in the *Detroit Free Press* announced: 'New Media Calls for New Majors.' The article describes the Electronic Critique Program (E-Crit) at the University of Detroit Mercy. E-Crit is an interdisciplinary program that combines English, Communications, Computer Information Systems, and Fine Art. The premise of the headline seems simple enough; given the rapid development of new technologies over the past few decades, a digital revolution that pervades every facet of our lives, universities must respond by offering a degree concentration in new media.[1] The simplicity of the premise, however, is an illusion. To suggest that new media call for new majors is to suggest that changes in technology require changes in academic curriculum; not just changes in course content, mind you, but an alteration in the very structure of the academic disciplinary system through the creation of a new degree program.

E-Crit was born out of the Frankfurt School / poststructural sensibility of two of my colleagues and their students, who positioned resistance and vigilant critique as the cornerstones in a new media studies curriculum that opposes the compartmentalization of knowledge. How this proposal made it by the university's conservative governing body shall remain a mystery. But the success of the proposal – which amounts to no more than institutionalizing a program that is critical of the institution – proves to me that a change in discourse, namely an effective combination of poststructural theory and technology, could induce a change in the larger, more unyielding structure of an institution. The goal, then, is to position discourse in such a way that it can play a formative role in reshaping the academic apparatus. As I hope to demonstrate through this book, Electronic Critique is not just the quirky name of an interdisciplinary degree program at the University of Detroit Mercy; it is a philosophy that can impact academic discourse, scholarly practices, pedagogy, and institutional structures at any university. This book is not about the degree program, but about the ideals on which it was founded and instituted.

From an economic perspective, some might say that the university's legitimization of E-Crit (which was initially proposed as a liberal arts curriculum with a focus on Web design) was a knee-jerk response to the 'dot.com' boom of the late 1990s. 'At last,' the university administration must have rejoiced, 'the humanities have found a way to be marketable once again.' The question of the marketability of the humanities is central to this book, and I draw heavily on the work of John Guillory, whose *Cultural Capital* provides a realistic analysis of the state of the humanities in techno-bureaucratic culture – a culture whose 'fetishization of "rigor"' has led to a veritable crisis in the humanities (ix). This crisis was temporarily allayed, according to Guillory, with the introduction of critical theory into the literary canon, which amounted to a perceived jolt of rigour for an otherwise valueless humanities curriculum. With the end of the 'age of theory' upon us, a moment underscored by Terry Eagleton in *After Theory*, it is crisis time once again. Or, more precisely, the crisis never really went away. In spite of the much too prevalent sense of entitlement and academic complacency typical of humanities research in North America, I think it's time to take a harder look at how disciplines rooted in the study and preservation of printed texts can remain relevant and viable in a digital, picture-oriented culture.

Given the brutal end of the '90s high-tech honeymoon, I am faced with a different, though related, crisis to the one mentioned above: what are the E-Crit graduates, humanities-educated technophiles, going to do in a market that has seen the end of high-paying Web design jobs and wildly successful IT start-ups? My usual, careful response to this question is that E-Crit no longer focuses exclusively on Web design, and that multimedia development, programming, and IT management in their various manifestations are not going away any time soon. Graduates will find employment in these areas. What is most likely is that they will invent new positions for themselves, either in established corporate environments or through entrepreneurial initiatives. But this is not how I would like to respond to the question How rigorous is E-Crit? or, more commonly, How practical is it? – a question I field regularly when meeting the parents of prospective students. What matters most, I would like to say, is that wherever the graduates find employment, they will challenge inhumane (or post-human, if you will) techno-bureaucratic practices and structures fostered by a marketplace that blindly values efficiency, reason, and financial gain above all else. But this flood of theory jargon would be no way to garner the support of university administration, let alone woo potential donors, or reassure the hand-wringing parents of incoming freshmen.

There is yet another reason why I don't offer this second (Marxist and poststructuralist) rejoinder. In many ways, I see this response as nostalgic, idealistic even, to the point of nausea. It is too easily allied to a 1960s sensibility that spawned not only hippies but deconstruction and cybernetics as well. Is it possible to be nostalgic about poststructuralism or deconstruction? Even as I write those conspicuous theory words, the rows of books on the shelves before me, volumes of varying sizes by Jacques Derrida, Michel Foucault et al., seem faded and ghostly, relics whose fate is to be digitally archived and buried forever in the humanities canon. Their time has passed, their promise, unfulfilled. What has happened, I ask, to the revolutionary potential of what is now summarized as postmodern theory? Was it really a fad after all?

One way of explaining this sense of disappointment in the 'failure of theory' is to investigate how attempts to apply deconstruction toward the materialization of revolutionary scholarly practices have been largely ineffectual. For example, the books on my shelf that fall under the rubric of 'hypertext theory' appear even more artefactual than the poststructural texts that were responsible for inspiring emancipatory musings on the convergence of contemporary critical theory and hypertext. What happened to deconstruction in the process of this technological turn? To put it simply, somewhere in the early 1990s, the major tenets of deconstruction (death of the Author, intertextuality, etc.) were displaced into technology, that is, hypertext. Or to put it another way, philosophy was transformed, liquidated even, into the materiality of new media. This alchemical transformation did not result in the creation of new, experimental scholarly methods that mobilize deconstruction via technology, but in an academic fever for digital archiving and accelerated hermeneutics, both of which replicate, and render more efficient, traditional scholarly practices that belong to the print apparatus.[2]

Following Michel Foucault, Gregory Ulmer defines the term 'apparatus' as 'an interactive matrix of technology, institutional practices, and ideological subject formation' (1994a: 17). We have had over five hundred years to understand the technology, institutional practices, and ideologies of the print apparatus, and some excellent studies can attest to this. However, with the encroachment of digital technology in academia, we have an opportunity to shape a new apparatus, and this involves more than transferring the old habits of scholarship into a multi-linear, electronic writing space. Shaping a new apparatus also involves more than a scholarly *remediation*[3] of printed texts. In *The Digital Revolution and the Coming of the Postmodern University*, Carl Raschke observes that 'today's typical college classroom, excluding perhaps its décor and architecture, does not look or function much differently from the way it did in the 1920s. Can one imagine any other crucial pillar of culture, or sector of the economy, that has not changed that much in eighty years?' (vii). This classroom example should be considered as a microcosm of what is at stake here. A large-scale institutional change of the type I am envisioning can only come about with a careful and deliberate implementation that targets not only the discourse of scholars, but that of students and classrooms (including ergonomics), administrators and buildings (including architecture), campuses and cities (including urban planning).

While it may sound strange to speak of discourse in these materialist terms, it is the failure of critics and philosophers to have a lasting, palpable impact that has led to what Terry Eagleton has called the end of 'the golden age of cultural theory' (2003: 1). According to Derrida,

> Following the consistency of its logic, it [deconstruction] attacks not only the internal edifice, both semantic and formal, of philosophemes, but also what one would be wrong to assign to it as its external housing, its extrinsic conditions of practice: the historical forms of its pedagogy, the social, economic, or political structures of this pedagogical institution. It is because deconstruction interferes with solid structures, 'material' institutions, and not only with discourses or signifying representations, that it is always distinct from an analysis or a 'critique.' (1987: 19)

This material component of critical theory seems to have lost its way in the past few decades. This book is about giving theory a new body so that it does more than lead to predictable readings of texts, whether those texts are canonical literature, a political event, or *The Simpsons*.

As I mention above, the Electronic Critique Program is not the subject of this book, but it serves as a case study for materializing the theories put forth here. The primary goal of this study is to reclaim deconstruction from the digital liquidation it underwent in the 1990s in order to apply it more carefully (though experimentally and radically) in the creation of discursive practices that are suitable to a culture that has embraced electronic technology and has internalized the primary tenets of postmodern theory, but has done so by way of popular culture and computing techniques. A large portion of this study involves an attempt to create a new method of scholarly research – which I have dubbed *hypericonomy* – that is more suitable to a picture-oriented, digital-centric culture. While this exercise in invention (what Gregory Ulmer would call *heuretics*) might not yield a perfectly replicable set of practices, it provides a strategic model of how the academic apparatus might be transformed by a reconfiguration of discursive practices. *E-Crit* is a glimpse at what 'knowledge production' might look like, after deconstruction, in an age of computer-mediated communication.

For this reason, this book covers a wide range of sites for potential revolution, from scholarly discourse, to pedagogical practices, to curricular structure, a strategy which differentiates it from most other new media texts. Scholars from any field can turn to this book for new research methods and pedagogical approaches that draw thoughtfully on the materiality of digital media. Students can turn to this book for renewed hope in the relevance and importance of a humanities education. For academic administrators, *E-Crit* might serve as a case study in an attempt to engage in meaningful curricular innovation. Finally, this book is for those who are concerned about the future of the humanities in a digital culture, and who seek to resist the dehumanization of higher education, which is carried out blindly in the name of 'technological progress.'

E-Crit

Digital Media, Critical Theory, and the Humanities

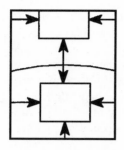

1. THE CANON, THE ARCHIVE, AND THE REMAINDER: Reimagining Scholarly Discourse

Just as a child who starts using words without yet understanding them, who adds more and more uncomprehended linguistic fragments to his playful activity, discovers the sense-giving principle only after he has been active in this way for a long time ... in the very same way the inventor of a new world view must be able to talk nonsense until the amount of nonsense created by him and his friends is big enough to give sense to all its parts.

– Paul Feyerabend, *Against Method*, 256–7

The Remainder: Structural, Material, Representational

There is something perverse about placing 'the remainder' at the beginning of a book. The leftovers are generally left to the conclusion, which is conventionally a container not only for summing things up, but also for alluding to all that could not possibly be said in the confines of the book. What facts or arguments have been neglected? What will be contested? What's next? These questions constitute the remainder of the study, the *other* of the thesis, that which has been left out, which could not be accommodated for reasons of materiality (a book can only be *so* long) and of ideology (opposing arguments could impede *my* argument). But in spite of any efforts to ignore it, the spectre of this remainder will always be present in any written text – or in any picture, for that matter[1] – and not even the seemingly infinite structure of a hypertext can exorcise this ghost completely. There will always be something left unsaid, something more to say. So there is no point in trying to say it all. In universities, students learn this lesson in expository writing classes, and their professors are haunted by it in the pursuit of academic publication. Good academic writing is achieved through a process of exclusion.

But there is another 'remainder' at play in academic writing, in spite of the ceaseless efforts of scholars to root it out. This second, more repressed, spectre is the subject of Jean-Jacques Lecercle's *The Violence of Language*, and it haunts this entire book. All of the linguistic tools that account for the poetics of this study – a poetics I have come to call *hypericonomy* – might be classified under what Jean-Jacques Lecercle has termed 'the remainder' of language. Puns, anagrams, false etymologies, macaronics, and metaphor of all breeds fall into this repressed category, this 'other of language' (99). More importantly here, the remainder is the 'other' of academic or scholarly language. It is deemed as nonsense or rubbish, classified as 'cute' or juvenile, the stuff of children's literature, fantasy, and folklore, and, lately, as unstylish poststructural writing. But the remainder cannot be repressed; it is proof positive that ghosts or monsters do exist, not just in the fantastic stories of children's books and science fiction, but in language itself. These monsters prey upon our linguistic fears and linger in our unconscious. 'The remainder,' according to Lecercle, 'is the realm of linguistic teratology, of false units and illicit constructions. Monsters, however, in addition to their obvious charm, have always been of the utmost interest to science, casting light as they do on the structure of normal phenomena' (60).

E-Crit attempts to take this teratological science a step further by viewing the 'remainder' not only as a means of illuminating conventional language, but as a language with a revolutionary potential of its own. If the remainder is the hidden or repressed, monstrous 'other' of the conventional academic discourse, then those who seek to change that conventional discourse might engage in a science of *anagnorisis*; that is, a science of invention and knowledge-production that depends on a face-to-face encounter with the monster.

Like Lecercle, the poet and literary critic Susan Stewart describes nonsense and sense as the two facets of a symbiotic affiliation: 'The two conceptions, the commonsensical and the nonsensical, ... are in a state of mutual implication; they are two sides of the same coin' (1978: 107). What has been left out in the ellipsis of this quotation is what makes Stewart's theory different from that of Lecercle. The ellipsis conceals the necessary political element of this relationship: the fact that common sense and nonsense are commensurate to the positions of 'the dominant and the dominated' (107). Like the relationship between common sense and nonsense, the relationship between scholarly, academic language and the remainder is that of master and slave. At the risk of falling into emancipatory rhetoric, it might be suggested that this book is an attempt to undo this relationship so that the remainder can occupy the foreground. One goal of this study is to let the monsters out of the dungeon, if only for a moment, and join in the games that they play.

Of course, there are risks involved in such an undertaking, as there are in any attempt to confront repression or oppression. I will avoid over-personifying this tale of linguistic slavery and its eradication, however, for the emancipation of the remainder has much less to do with Alex Haley's *Roots* than it does with the 'roots' of Gilles Deleuze and Félix Guattari. Even so, as this chapter demonstrates, those who seek to liberate the remainder will face political resistance, ideological dismissal, and even personal denigration. By speaking of the remainder in these political terms, as a case of exclusion, repression, and otherness, I am hoping to supplement John Guillory's important study of canon formation in *Cultural Capital*. As Guillory reveals in his introduction, *Cultural Capital* is not really about canon formation, that is, the 'canon debate' that has plagued literary studies for the past two decades. Rather than joining the debate about what should and shouldn't be canonized, he turns to what he calls the '*impensé* of the debate,' namely, the category of literature itself, or the formation of the concept of literature and the capital value of literary study in a techno-scientific culture. Guillory suggests that the canon is nothing more than a product of the scholarly imaginary, and that the debate points essentially to a crisis in the humanities wrought by a fetishistic clinging to traditional conceptions of literature and scholarship. This is the fate of literary studies in universities dominated by a techno-bureaucratic culture that values 'rigor'[2] above all else.

What Guillory proposes in response to the crisis is an analysis of the institutional practices that determine the meaning of 'literature,' without which the canon debate and the creation of non-canonical, emancipatory syllabi would be impossible. In Guillory's terms,

> It is only in the pedagogic imaginary that changing the syllabus means in any *immediate* sense changing the world; what is required now is an analysis of the institutional location and mediation of such imaginary structures as the canon in order to first assess the real effects of the imaginary, and then to bring the imaginary itself under more strategic political control. (37)

While Guillory focuses primarily on the permutations of the category of 'literature,' this study is more concerned with the category of 'academic writing,' which is the primary vehicle for mediating the 'imaginary structures' of higher education. As Guillory suggests, the ideology of literary tradition that is at the root of the canon debate is always 'a history of writers and not of *writing*' (63). Guillory is interested, therefore, in how writing becomes literature. This study, however, asks how writing becomes scholarship, and it does so not only by examining the practices and structures of the academic apparatus, but also by imagining a new method of scholarly writing (hypericonomy) and a new curricular strategy (Electronic Critique). In the following chapters, then, I move from scholarly writing to pedagogy and curriculum, providing a holistic strategy for re-imagining the academic apparatus in the context of a techno-scientific culture where the humanities have lost their market value. We begin, in this chapter, with a case study in the practices and structures that determine the boundaries of scholarly writing.

Four years ago, I submitted a hypertext essay, 'A Provisional Treatment for Archive Fever,' to a Web-based humanities journal. The essay was solicited by a guest-editor who saw me present a paper on the topic at an international conference. When I submitted the hypertext, the journal editor received it with gratitude and enthusiasm. The journal referees, however, were not so enthusiastic upon first reviewing the hypertext, and the work was not accepted for publication. Admittedly, some of their comments were quite reasonable, especially those regarding my use of 'cyber jargon' and my frequent lapses into a bombastic, perhaps *techno-manifesto-ish*, tone (we were at the apex of the 'dot.com' boom, after all). I edited the essay in the hope of correcting these tonal mishaps, and I submitted it to another journal on the recommendation of the editor, to whom I am grateful.[3] I am even more grateful, however, to that editor's team of referees, whose comments largely reflected the unconventional methodology employed in the hypertext – these were the editorial recommendations that I chose not to follow, for they had a direct bearing on the ideological intent of the project. Their comments have provided me with an organizational structure for investigating conventional academic discourse and its remainder.

Since the essay I submitted to the journal was non-traditional from an academic perspective, the referees' comments, as reproduced here, should act as a sort of warning for the inventors of new modes of academic discourse; namely, this is what to expect when you submit 'remainder-work' to a traditional journal. More importantly, the referees' comments supply the raw material of an instruction book on how to write with the remainder. The following sections are organized according to excerpts from the referees' comments – comments in which the remainder crops up quite frequently. Each excerpt demonstrates an instance of resistance to three different types of remainder in scholarly discourse, some of which are identified here as 'remainders' for the very first time. The first type of remainder is taken directly from Lecercle and Deleuze/Guattari, and it relates to the rhizomatic principle of structure[4] disdained by traditional, *rigorous* humanities scholars: the *structural remainder*. The second type is more grammatological in nature; it concerns the repressed technological element of humanities scholarship, and the resistance of scholars to certain communications technologies: the *material remainder*. The third type of remainder, which is closely allied to the second, accounts for a great deal of the theoretical writing in this book: the *representational remainder* of scholarly discourse, which might also be termed the *pictorial remainder*.

Tree vs. Roots – Structural Remainder

Referee's comment: 'Leaps via pun are ... cute and confusing.'

The idea that a pun can leap, or act as a vehicle for leaping, is certainly worthy of any of the works of Lewis Carroll (imagine a little girl bouncing on a pun-go stick), especially if that pun or leap is 'cute.' What is being proposed in the referee's comment is that the logic of connection employed in the hypertext essay was objectionable because it relied not on conventional, logical, sequential progression, but on what Gregory Ulmer has called 'the puncept' (1989). In punceptual writing, data is organized according to the logic of the pun, the most base and primitive species of remainder; punning is what makes the work of Marshall McLuhan, for example, both brilliant and annoying. By drawing on the pun as a means of organization, a research program can be carried into fields of inquiry which may be pertinent to the study, but otherwise ignored or excluded due to a conventional commitment to 'relevance'[5] or specialization. The linking of the film *Roots* (which crops up again in a later chapter) with Deleuze and Guattari's 'rhizome' theory is an example of the puncept at work. Not only does this *leap* allow me to link the literal, historical notion of slavery to the theoretical, abstract concept of the remainder, but by cutting across types of media and cultural artefacts, this pun-work can lead toward other areas of investigation – sociocultural, autobiographical, racial, technological – that a study of the remainder should explore. Most importantly, perhaps, this *Roots* pun is a mnemonic device, reminding us of the physical violence[6] that language can inflict when taken to the extreme of oppressive discipline.

As I will attempt to demonstrate in the following chapters of this study, the puncept can also be pictorial. The art of Stephen Gibb, pictured throughout this book, provides an entire thesis on the subject, which is the guiding premise of hypericonomy, a mode of discourse organized according to the pictorial pun. Among the visual puns employed in this study is that of the tree, a pervasive symbol of traditional print-centric scholarship, instituted (though not invented) by Peter Ramus and carried forward by Ben Jonson, William Blake, Roland Barthes, and others discussed here. Deleuze and Guattari mobilize the tree as a hypericon at several instances in their investigation of the rhizome,[7] as does Lecercle: 'Like the tree, the rhizome is more than an image – it is a concept. It has, therefore, distinct characteristics' (1990: 132). While Lecercle is certainly touching upon the iconic ('more than an image – it is a concept') value of the rhizome here, what matters most is that he is able to link the characteristics of the rhizome with those of the remainder, characteristics which Deleuze and Guattari call 'Principles' (1987).

The first principle of the rhizome to which Lecercle alludes is the principle of connection:

A point in the rhizome can be connected with any other point. There are no fixed paths, as in a tree. The remainder is unstructured: in the matter of relationships, anything goes, be it proximity, phonic similarity, or obsessional recurrence. The remainder has no master root, no centre: its relationships are eccentric. (1990: 133)

Here we can see how the rhizomatic principle of connection which character-izes remainder-work also describes the punceptual structuring principle of hypericonomy, as practised in the following chapters. Hypericonomy emu-lates the structural characteristic of the rhizome by foregrounding the remain-der in scholarly research and writing. The pun, then, even though it may be deemed as 'cute' or 'confusing' to those who are unaccustomed to its rhizo-matic ways, can be used as a structuring tool in a scholarly research program.

Print vs. Electronic – Material Remainder

Referee's comment: 'It seems to me that this essay needs to be put into conventional essay form, so that a thesis is clearly stated and key terms defined, before it goes deconstructive.'

Hypericonomy is not only motivated by a need for political and disciplinary change, but also by a recognition of the potential of new media to enhance scholarship. As too many scholars have argued, new media seem to provide us with a remarkably suitable space for a deconstructive praxis. Perhaps this is why, in the comment above, the referee fuses or confuses the notion of 'going deconstructive' with 'going electronic.' If, in the referee's commen-tary, there is an unconscious echo of 'going bad,' 'going crazy,' 'going postal,' 'going ballistic,' etc., it is only because language is rearing its violent head once again. According to the referee, the unconventional, hypertextual struc-ture of the essay thwarts the clarity of the argument and frustrates his/her desire for a 'clearly stated thesis.' The recommended solution is to write the essay in a 'conventional essay form' before rendering it in hypertext. The problem, however, is that this request is emerging from a print-oriented agenda, whereas the essay was written in and for a digital culture. The hypertext essay was not proposing a single argument, but rather a 'structure of possibilities' (Bolter 1991: 119). It was, after all, an experimental piece call-ing for humanities researchers to draw on new media for formal experimen-tation, rather than drawing on them solely as a means of increasing the efficiency of traditional scholarly practices: archiving and interpretation. My submission was, to borrow Lev Manovich's term, an attempt to write (in) the *language of new media.* The suggestion that it should be 'put into conventional essay form ... before it goes deconstructive' is indicative of the referee's oppressive print-centricity.

The referee's recommendation ignores the possible connection between technologies of writing and modes of cognition, the possibility that new media might produce their own visual rhetoric, or might even alter print-based modes of writing through a process of what Jay Bolter and Richard Grusin have called 'remediation.' It has become tiresome and redundant to reiterate the notion that we are on the verge of a highly pictorial, electronic, post-print culture. There is a vast discrepancy between conventional scholarly procedures and contemporary modes of storage, recall, and representation. Once this discrepancy is recognized on a large scale, then digital-centric standards of evaluation will be applied to essays submitted to supposedly digital-centric journals. But until that recognition is realized, academia is faced with an inevitable anachronism.

The real problem in this conflict of writing technologies is one of ideological incompatibility: I submitted a digital-oriented research project to a print-oriented (though digital) journal. As I will argue throughout this book, it is a definitive characteristic of traditional scholars to reject any mode of discourse that diverges from the path of the conventional, hierarchical essay format. It should not come as a surprise that the overwhelming majority of scholarly Web sites are merely Web-based translations of printed journals, designed according to the print-centric logic of the hard-copy versions. What's more, those scholarly sites that claim to be most innovative in their use of the materiality of the Web relegate themselves to the task of archiving (this is the subject of the hypertext essay I submitted). In an attempt to temper the 'softness' of digital data, they bind their archives with warnings about copyright infringement, and obsess over whether or not the digital copies of images provide an accurate depiction of the print copies.[8] These sites are intended for a single purpose: to provide a more quick and efficient way for scholars to produce predictable, print-centric essays.

Figure 1.1, depicting the structure of the Pennsylvania Electronic Edition of Mary Shelley's *Frankenstein*, provides an apt example of how an appropriate scholarly hypertext should be structured. Clearly, the monstrous subject of this project is not reflected in its structure. Put simply, there just aren't enough arrows. This scholarly hypertext, like so many others, involves a prodigious effort of transcription and archiving, but it does not make full use of the rhizomatic potential of electronic writing. If a digital project is not organized according to the tree structure dictated by print technology, then it has very little chance of succeeding in traditional academic circles. This might lead one to believe that scholarship, or at least humanities scholarship, and its latest instantiation, 'Digital Humanities,' is suffering from a severe strain of 'archive fever.'[9] Although Derrida does not use the expression in this exact context, he describes this viral strain as 'a compulsive, repetitive, and nostalgic desire for the archive, an irrepressible desire to return to the origin, a homesickness, a nostalgia for the return to the most archaic place of absolute commencement' (1996: 91). In the mid-1990s, after George P. Landow proclaimed the 'convergence of hypertext and literary theory,' traces of this terminal archival strain could be diagnosed nearly everywhere in the body of humanities scholarship. Take, for example, this description of the feverish labour involved in compiling the Pennsylvania Electronic Edition of Mary Shelley's *Frankenstein*:

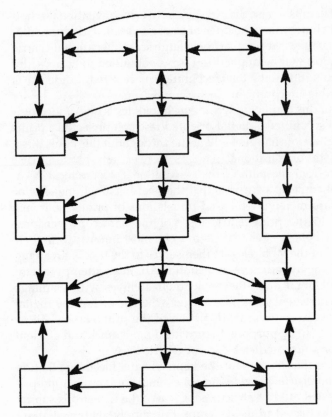

1.1 Structure of the Pennsylvania Electronic Edition of Mary Shelley's *Frankenstein*.

> Although getting our hands on all of this and scanning or typing it has been daunting, we've tried to include everything we can, without regard to traditional notions of canonicity. The lot is complemented with factual material on science, philosophy, politics, history. Dozens of short essays on the history of polar expeditions, electricity, spontaneous generation, and the like situate the reader in the nineteenth century, while two hundred capsule biographies introduce the most important figures surrounding the novel. (Lynch 1997)

By all means, this edition is an admirable accomplishment, and humanities scholars owe a great debt of gratitude to these and all the archons of the digital age who work feverishly to transfer documents from one medium to another. I have done such work myself; *Être en mal d'archive*, it seems, means not only 'to have archive fever,' but also 'to be in need of archives' (Derrida 1996: 91). Indeed, this entire book would have been radically different, or even impossible, had I not had access to a variety of digital archives.

However, although digital technologies provide us with the most effective archiving tools to date, archiving should not be the defining task of digital humanities scholars. In these archival projects, scholars are using only a portion of the potential of new media; it is the portion which most appeases: (a) their nostalgia for a print-oriented culture; and (b) the demands of a digital-oriented, techno-bureaucratic culture that values predictable techno-scientific methods (e.g., archiving) over interpretation and, most of all, invention. If humanities scholars do not make a concerted effort to relinquish traditional definitions of literature and scholarship, their professional destiny will be that of 'digital archivist,' and their success will be measured by the size of their supposedly canon-undermining archive projects. Remediating the canon requires a concerted focus on the materiality of writing, and not on the writers themselves.

Text vs. Picture – Representational Remainder

Referee's comment: 'In general, the essay has wonderful potential as an essay about how readings of canonical texts might be changed by adding images.'

When, in the opening paragraph of her adventures in Wonderland, Alice asks, 'What is the use of a book ... without pictures or conversations?' this is not the naïve complaint of a spoiled and lazy child suffering from mid-afternoon ennui (Carroll 1963: 25). This rhetorical question is as complex and philosophical as the White Knight's seemingly Derridian song of infinite digression in *Through the Looking Glass*.[10] As I will demonstrate throughout this study, pictures are a sort of remainder vis-à-vis traditional scholarship. A picture is a remainder not only in the sense of being a suppressed or neglected element of conventional academic discourse – the representational *other* of rigorous academic discourse – but also in the sense that pictures, in the form of personal memories, patterns of organization, cultural artefacts, are always at work in the repressed background of any scholarly program. In the world of scholarship today, the picture is 'not a shady verso to a rightful recto. It is rather like one's shadow: a constant companion, which one tends to forget, but whose absence – conceivable only in tales of the uncanny – would be sorely missed' (Lecercle 1990: 99).

In this context, the suggestion that 'readings of canonical texts might be changed by adding images' seems like a vast oversimplification and a misunderstanding of the place of pictorial representation in scholarship. This comment expresses an archetypal scholarly attitude toward pictures: from the conventional point of view, pictures are entities to be 'added' to an essay or lesson, and not inherent or repressed elements of the processes of writing, reading, and learning. In this particular case, pictures are seen as elements which might change 'readings of canonical texts,' but not as elements which might altogether change the *processes* of reading and writing. To relegate pictures to the task of 'changing readings of canonical texts' is to enter them, quite safely, into circulation with conventional scholarly discourse. The ultimate purpose of pictures, according to this view, is to enhance or embellish the hermeneutic circle of traditional scholarly writing.

On several occasions in this study, the term 'heuretics,' borrowed from Gregory Ulmer, will be used to describe a supplementary or alternative logic to hermeneutic discourse, a way out of the hermeneutic circle. In short, heuretics provides us with a logic of invention, 'a form of generative productivity of the sort practiced in the avant-garde' (Ulmer 1994a: xii). What I am attempting to outline in this book is a heuretic approach to discourse that draws on the suggestive power of pictures as a means of generating new modes of writing suitable to an image-oriented culture. As generative instruments, pictures are extremely productive. A picture tends to *speak with less authority than words*; it is not subject to the same, rigid rule-set, and therefore it is more capable of generating divergent cognitive responses from the viewer. Hypericonomy works by unearthing and foregrounding those divergent responses which would otherwise be repressed in the course of conducting scholarly research. The purpose of this foregrounding, however, is not to interpret the picture, or to offer an authoritative *reading* of it in the conventional sense, but to draw on the picture as a tool for invention, as a generator of concepts and linkages unavailable to conventional scholarly practices. This is how hypericonomy breaks out of the hermeneutic circle.

Of course, pictures are not the only potential generators of these divergent research materials, and it is appropriate that a theorist named Lecercle (the circle) would be the one to show us how words can help break the circle as well. Words have a generative potential of their own. We have already seen how the pun, for example, can create unconventional, yet informative, linkages between concepts. Still, pictures seem to possess a greater propensity for facilitating remainder-work, and for generating divergent responses. This fact is well understood in the world of advertising.

To understand pictures as generators is to view them much in the same way as Lecercle describes the pun and other forms of metaphor, all of which fall into the category of the remainder, which Lecercle describes as instances of 'diachrony-within-synchrony.' This term, as perplexing as it is at first sight, is rendered more familiar in the following chapters, where it is identified as one of the essential elements of hypericonomy. The notion of 'diachrony-within-synchrony' points to the capacity of the remainder to interrupt our synchronic understanding of a word by invoking a diachronic association. The punning use of 'vise/vice/de-vise/vis' in chapter 3 is a sufficient example of how a diachronic understanding of a word can interrupt its most literal, synchronic definition. By means of the pun, etymology, and macaronics, 'the rigid insulation of synchrony from diachrony is threatened by a short circuit whereby history is reinscribed in the present' (Lecercle 1990: 187). Pictures can produce the same effect of 'diachrony-within-synchrony,' as I have also attempted to demonstrate in chapter 3 by creating an iconography of the vise. As a pictorial pun, the vise can be diachronically transformed into a printing press, the brackets in a set of Ramist dichotomies, and the hands of William Blake's Nurse, all of which play a seminal role in the chapter. In hypericonomy, the effect of 'diachrony-within-synchrony' permits researchers to cut across a diversity of discourse networks in order to chart networks of their own.

The concept of 'diachrony-within-synchrony' can be further elucidated by what Lecercle calls 'indirection':

> 'Indirection' means that the process of interpretation, or production, goes both ways indifferently. All the possible meanings of a metaphorical phrase are present at once, without the order they are given in a dictionary, which is normally based on historical principles and treats the 'literal' meaning as primary. (1990: 174)

Both the reader of a metaphorical phrase and the viewer of a picture must control this sense of indirection (which, incidentally, might lead him/her into esoteric directions not found 'in a dictionary'). Those familiar with schizophrenia will understand why this control must be present: without the ability to filter or funnel information into a single direction – the 'good' or 'common' direction (*sens*) – the viewer or listener will be overwrought by an onslaught of stimuli, and eventually deemed mad by the purveyors of good sense.[11] This funnelling of stimuli is an unconscious operation, present whenever an individual is faced with a visual or verbal proposition. But it may be possible to capture or at least re-create this sense of schizo 'indirection' before it is funnelled, before it is transformed into common sense. 'In the genesis of every proposition,' Lecercle tells us,

> there is a moment of creation, of potential nonsense, but also of fluidity: the moment of sense before a (self-)conscious subject takes over, before the world is designated, before *langue* with its fixed units and general rules imposes its structure on language. This moment of sense is obliterated when good sense wins. (1990: 178)

A study published in the September 2003 issue of the *Journal of Personality and Social Psychology* strengthens this proposition by suggesting that there is a link between creative individuals and a process called 'latent inhibition,' which echoes the 'funnelling' concept I invoke above. According to researchers at the University of Toronto and at Harvard University, creative individuals are likely to have lower levels of latent inhibition, and are therefore able to 'remain in contact with extra information constantly streaming in from the environment' (Carson et al. 2003). I would argue that it may be possible to teach creativity by providing individuals with an apparatus for knowledge-building that allows them to maintain access to a more diverse range of information. While I would like to make this claim for hypericonomy, my goal is not to dabble in cognitive psychology, but to create a mode of discourse more suitable to our culture of information overload. In any case, I would like to believe that one purpose of hypericonomy is to provoke or mimic the fluidity of creative thought and crystallize it, transforming *délire* or schizophrenia into a theory and a discursive practice.

The Good Sense of Nonsense

I have now crossed the frontier into Gilles Deleuze's understanding of sense, and his punning of that term with the French word *sens* or 'direction.' Without going too far beyond this frontier, I would simply note that sense, according to Deleuze, is present in every utterance, even in so-called *nonsense*, which should not be understood as a lack of sense (or direction) at all, but as an overproduction of sense (indirection = too many directions at once, no single direction). 'From the point of view of structure,' Deleuze suggests, 'there is always too much sense: an excess produced and over-produced by nonsense' (1969: 71). It is in this sense that the language of new media, with its multi-discursive, diachronic structure, is nonsensical. If 'good sense affirms that in all things there is a determinable sense or direction (*sens*)' (Deleuze 1969: 1), then new media allow us to take the crooked path(s) of nonsense, refusing to lay out a single path for all things.

What remains to be considered in this theory of sense, however, is this: When it comes to scholarly discourse, *who* is determining the sense? Who is pointing us in the direction of *good* scholarly sense and, more importantly, *why*? According to Deleuze, 'the systematic characteristics of good sense' might be described in this way:

> ... it affirms a single direction; it determines this direction to go from the most to the least differentiated, from the singular to the regular, and from the remarkable to the ordinary; it orients the arrow of time from past to future, according to this determination; it assigns to the present a directing role in this orientation; it renders possible thereby the function of prevision; and it selects the sedentary type of distribution in which all of the preceding characteristics are brought together. (1969: 76)

With a few minor adjustments, this description of 'good sense' might very well be mistaken for a description of traditional scholarly discourse, a mode of discourse which organizes all data according to a pre-visioned, synchronic hierarchy, a 'sedentary type of distribution' in which all 'relevant' data may be easily organized into a single, homogeneous argument. The

1.2 Stephen Gibb, *This Is Not a Pipe Dream*, 1998.

Republic of Scholars, which I will define more carefully in the next chapter, manufactures good sense as it exists in the academic world today, and those who wish to challenge this understanding of good sense must be aware of what they are up against.

The *who* of good sense is obvious, then, and the *why* might be answered by pointing to the history and tradition of scholarly discourse, with its roots in early print technology and the structure of the first universities. But there are other, more political, more confrontational answers to this why of scholarly discourse, which have to do with the unlikely coupling of traditionalists who seek to maintain a certain complacent, bourgeois, academic status quo, and techno-bureaucratic university administrators seeking to run a viable business.

Electronic critique, though it may not ever be accepted as 'good sense,' is at least a step toward redefining academic sense and nonsense, a step in the right direction, which is also a step toward indirection. My hope is that this study, as nonsensical as it is at times, will provide the reader with an education on how to mobilize the remainder in the transformation of the academic apparatus, and that it might provoke, at least for a moment, the possibility that 'suddenly, something new happens, a proposition "makes sense" in an original manner – a moment that has long been lost in the passage to "good" or "common" sense' (Lecercle 1990: 177). Finally, if there is to be a slogan for such an educational program, it must be stolen from Deleuze and Guattari: 'Don't sow, grow offshoots!' In such a case, common sense, the right direction, would be poly-direction, a sense with multiple offshoots, multiple roads; a network of paths interlinking words and pictures, departments and campuses, cultures and polities, neurons and electrons. Then again, I may be better off abandoning such emancipatory rhetoric and leave the reader instead with a picture (fig. 1.2), a hypericon that encapsulates much of what I have proposed already, and will continue to develop throughout the following chapters.

2. THE SEARCH FOR EXEMPLARS: Discourse Networks and the Pictorial Turn

Indeed, if after the death of God (Nietzsche), the end of grand Narratives of Enlightenment (Lyotard), and the arrival of the Web (Tim Berners-Lee), the world appears to us as an endless and unstructured collection of images, texts, and other data records, it is only appropriate that we would want to develop a poetics, aesthetics, and ethics of this database.

– Lev Manovich, *The Language of New Media*, 219

Hypericon

The eye is battered and worn, simultaneously crying and sweating, hemmed in hopelessly by a threatening swarm of circuits, chips, and switches. Unlike its filmic predecessor, the scene of ocular torture in Stephen Gibb's *Eye Socket* (fig. 2.1) does not involve a razor blade, but a menacing three-pronged plug that looms serpent-like, waiting to be 'jacked in.' This is not the surrealist eye of a modernist culture, then, but the cyborgian eye of a culture more picture-oriented than Luis Buñuel might have ever conceived; a culture that has internalized the hypervisual, experimental images of the surrealists to such an extreme degree that their trace is visible everywhere, from mouse pads to children's books.[1] Stephen Gibb's *Eye Socket* or *Bronche l'oeil*, a painting that seems to have been designed exclusively for digital reproduction, demonstrates that the surrealist edge has cut deeply enough into our culture to be replicated with cartoonish simplicity, and distributed instantly to an audience of millions via the World Wide Web.

In spite of the apparently dilettantish style of Gibb's picture, one must not underestimate its potential to act as an important cultural signpost. Even though *Eye Socket* is not *Las meninas* (the painting that encapsulates Foucault's thesis in *The Order of Things*), it still provokes many questions for the willing observer, and is capable of launching a vast critical inquiry. *Eye Socket* is an

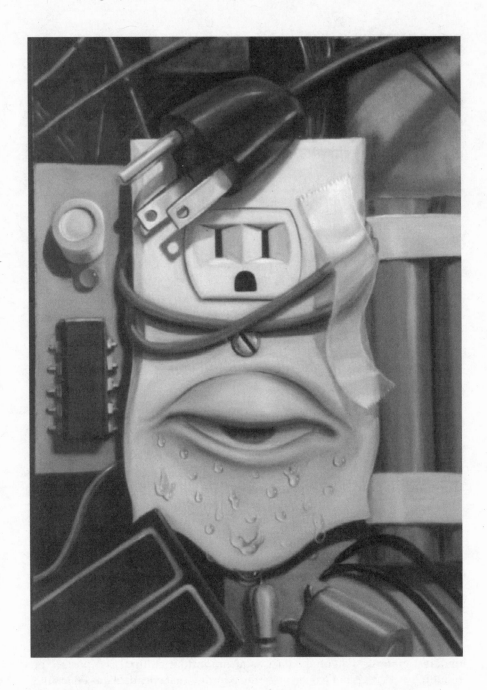

2.1 Stephen Gibb, *Eye Socket* or *Bronche l'oeil*, 1989.

image as ambivalent as the phrase 'plug the plug in the plug.' The viewer is invited to guess what lies at the other end of the tri-pronged cord. What invisible appliance threatens at any moment to be jacked in, wired for action? You might also ask whether the prongs will insert themselves into the outlet at all, or if they seek instead to gouge the captive eyeball, sacrificing, in a post-human libation, organic tissue for machine power.

Following in the tradition of surrealism and the grotesque, *Eye Socket* taunts us into a nonsensical line of interrogation. And we are indeed dealing with nonsense here, the irrational product of fantasy, the stuff of children's books and surrealist film. Typically, we might ask: In what type of world could such an object exist? Better yet, what are the conditions – social, psychological, material – that brought me into contact with this object? To pose this second question is to launch a completely different type of interrogation, one that seeks to locate the work within a complex field of possibilities. The goal might not be to determine a single origin for the painting (who painted it?), or to provide an authoritative explanation (why did he/she paint it?), but to establish the painting as a node onto a web of epistemes, or information circuits, if you will. In this way, the painting interrogates culture, rather than vice versa.

We might approach a picture, then, not as an entity worthy of study in and for itself, but as a node that provides access onto various currents of information. In this case, pictures are not just pictures, but discursive inlets and outlets. They are machines for generating theories, or even theories in themselves. The picture itself, when subjected to this approach, acts as a site for investigating the information networks that made it possible. *Eye Socket*, with its cyborgian electrical *outlets*, provides us with a fine mnemonic device. Consider the Gibb picture above, then, as the *limen*, the enchanted looking glass, between a network of discourses and the discourse on networks that I am developing here. In this context, *Eye Socket* has now become a 'hypericon': 'a piece of moveable cultural apparatus, one which may serve a marginal role as illustrative device or a central role as a kind of summary image ... that encapsulates an entire episteme, a theory of knowledge' (Mitchell 1994: 49). This chapter is designed to serve as a discussion of picture theory and discourse networks, with the intention of providing the reader with a series of exemplars for constructing a new mode of academic discourse.

Discourse Networks

Language, according to Michel Foucault,

is to thought and to signs what algebra is to geometry: it replaces the simultaneous comparison of parts (or magnitudes) with an order whose degrees must be traversed one after the other. It is in this strict sense that language is an analysis of thought: not a simple patterning, but a profound establishment of order in space. (Foucault 1994: 83)

Language, or to use a term preferred by Foucault, discourse, delivers order into an otherwise chaotic realm of signs. And when language is recorded in writing, seized indefinitely from the mutability of time, the potential for chaos is abated – at least according to a certain print-centric episteme that reached its height in the eighteenth century and continues to circulate today. This is the episteme of what Friedrich Kittler has called the Republic of Scholars, a republic entirely committed to 'endless circulation, a discourse network without producers or consumers, which simply heaves words around' (Kittler 1990: 4). It is this form of scholarly discourse, this discursive circuit, which renders itself visible through the production of banal treatises and dissertations. And it is this production line that I am attempting to expose and subsequently short-circuit here, even if such a short-circuiting must come at the cost of producing yet one more dissertation, and one more arsenal of footnotes.

'German poetry,' Friedrich Kittler informs us in the very first sentence of *Discourse Networks 1800/1900*, 'begins with a sigh' (3). Certainly, this is not the straightforward statement, the typical reiteration of received wisdom, that a reader might expect to encounter at the beginning of a scholarly text. One might assume that a poetic movement could begin with a war, a plague, a social upheaval of some sort, but not with a sigh. The pronouncement is almost surrealist in nature. There is no historical contextualization here, no precedent cited, no footnote, no doxical canting of objective proof. Even the most ardent postmodernist would protest that a rigorous theoretician would not make such a deterministic, grandiose statement about 'beginnings' – especially about the beginning of something as elusive and vast as 'German poetry.' This is not a scholarly statement at all; this is a rash reductionism, an imprudent trope, nonsense *tout court*. And this is exactly the way that we, as members of the Republic of Scholars, should react toward the first sentence of *Discourse Networks 1800/1900*. After all, this book was printed in and for a scholarly network of information delivery, and thus it is our right and duty to respond to it, write commentary, dissert, reiterate our expectations.

What we might expect instead of Kittler's nonsensical pronouncement is a logical outline, a historical rationalization that might possibly (though it is unlikely) eventually (after a series of proofs based on authoritative sources) lead up to the statement 'German poetry begins with a sigh.' But we are not dealing with a conventional scholarly text here; or, rather, we are not dealing with a text that flows smoothly along the circuit of scholarly discourse. Clearly, the first sentence of *Discourse Networks* is an instance of short-circuiting, as is Faust's sigh, for both interrupt the hermeneutic language of scholarship, which I will henceforth refer to as the *discourse of the Republic of Scholars*.

Although Kittler may seem unmistakably Foucauldian in his terminology (the term 'discourse network' encapsulates Foucault's archaeological methodology[2] in a single blow), his genealogy of scholarship does not correspond exactly to the episteme of classical scholarship archaeologized in *The Order of Things*. As David Wellbery has observed, 'Kittler chose to use the older system of erudition, the *res publica litteraria*,[3] rather than the classical episteme of transparent representation as the contrasting configuration to Romanticism' (1990: xx). The term 'Republic of Scholars,' then, designates a tradition of biblical exegesis or 'translation' rooted in Luther's dictum of *sola scriptura*.[4] This dictum calls for an objective, word-by-word recounting of scripture, which, according to Kittler, was fatally thwarted by a Romantic sigh, a verbal manifestation of the translator's soul. Kittler's decision to concentrate on this particularly reductive scholarly tradition seems appropriate given the current state of theory and criticism, which I will examine below. To put it in the bluntly economic terms of Katherine Hayles, we are in a situation of 'too many critics, too few texts,' and the result has not been innovation, but repetition, recycling, and reduction. As a solution to this problem, Hayles suggests her own version of Faust's sigh:

> Theory, with generalizations distilled from personal encounters with texts, can stimulate scholars to read old texts in new ways and seek out new texts that cannot be adequately understood without the theory. Maybe now is a good time for a double-braided text where the generalities of theory and the particularities of personal experience can both speak, though necessarily in different voices. A text where both voices can be heard, at first very different but then gradually coming closer until finally they are indistinguishable. (2002: 106)

This autobiographical approach, which falls in line with the classical academic credo of 'know thyself,' is certainly part of the scholarly method that I propose here. But the notion of a 'double-braid' in itself seems reductive. I would prefer to see a mode of scholarship that is more akin to an electrical cord, with its multiple, conductive circuits. In any case, to quibble over the 'incompleteness' of Kittler's contextualizing, the looseness with which the term 'Republic of Scholars' is used, his misunderstanding or abuse of Goethe's text, indicates that we, trained in hermeneutics, have overlooked the heuretic[5] potential of his innovative methodology. It is to this inventive, multi-braided potential in Kittler's work that I will now turn.

If we adhere to the demands of conventional literary scholarship, our reaction to Kittler's first chapter might be to acknowledge his discovery of a specific origin of German poetry, and inscribe this moment in the history of literary criticism, further supplementing our archive of tomes 'gnawed by worms, covered with dust' [Den Wurme nagen, Staub bedeckt] (Goethe 1990: 95, l.403). What's more likely, a traditional scholar might spurn Kittler's proposal altogether, and protest its lack of historical rigour. But an alternative reaction – the one I am supporting here – would be to recognize Kittler's methodology as a new way of conducting humanities research, a new method in which a specific scene or textual image (e.g., Faust's sigh, Gibb's *Eye Socket*, *Las meninas*) acts as a hypericon, a generative, multi-directional passageway onto a research project.

The notion that a single image or textual scene might act as an inlet onto a network of discourses is certainly not a new idea. The playful, deconstructive approach of Jacques Derrida and the structural experimentation of Roland Barthes have nearly put the term 'intertextuality' into everyday usage. Foucault sums up the concept rather aptly in *The Archaeology of Knowledge*, employing terms that are particularly suitable to this study:

> The frontiers of a book are never clear-cut: beyond the title, the first lines, and the last full stop, beyond its internal configuration and its autonomous form, it is caught up in a system of references to other books, other texts, other sentences: it is a node within a network ... The book is not simply the object that one holds in one's hands; and it cannot remain within the little parallelepiped that contains it: its unity is variable and relative. As soon as one questions that unity, it loses its self-evidence; it indicates itself, constructs itself, only on the basis of a complex field of discourse. (1971: 23)

It is this constructivist understanding of the text that spawned such notions as 'the death of the author,' and that led to such deconstructive *écriture*[6] as that found in Derrida's *Glas* and Barthes's *S/Z*. These experimental forms of discourse threatened to violently disrupt the traditional hermeneutic circuit of the Republic of Scholars in the 1960s and '70s. But their integration into the literary canon, as John Guillory outlines in an entire chapter of *Cultural Captial*, has only served to generate additional predictable commentaries, rather than spurring a transformation of literary critical methods.

In the words of Terry Eagleton, 'those who can, think up feminism or structuralism. Those who can't, apply such insights to *Moby-Dick* or *The Cat in the Hat*' (2003: 2). The experimental deconstructive texts of Derrida and Barthes (*Glas*, *S/Z*, etc.) – alienated by the cult of genius that has been imposed upon their authors–are to be observed as mere curiosities, commented upon, and filtered into theoretical dogma used to produce conventional 'readings' of other texts. But these experimental works have yet to be taken up as the roots of a discursive revolution in academia. As Eagleton observes,

> The older generation [of critical theorists] proved a hard act to follow. No doubt the new century will in time give birth to its own clutch of gurus. For the moment, however, we are still trading on the past – and this is a world which has changed dramatically since Foucault and Lacan first settled to their typewriters. What kind of fresh thinking does the new era demand? (2003: 2)

Eagleton's reference to the typewriter is perhaps an indication that today's 'gurus' might turn instead to the keyboard and mouse for inspiration. I would suggest that the new era demands thinking about the ways in which new media have impacted, and will continue to impact, literary theory. For this reason, Friedrich Kittler, an electrical engineer turned critical theorist, serves as an excellent exemplar of the type of 'fresh thinking' demanded by the new era. Although it's likely that most humanities scholars would shun the idea that in their spare time they should 'pick up the soldering iron and build circuits' (quoted in Griffin 1996: 731).[7]

Kittler attempts to force a meeting among canonical literary texts, the materiality of communication, and poststructural theory, one sample of which is *Discourse Networks 1800/1900*, an alchemical collision of seemingly immiscible elements. Although Kittler does not experiment much on a formal, material basis (as I have attempted to do, somewhat prudishly, throughout this book), he does indeed write in a 'post-hermeneutic' mode in which the concept of intertextuality exists as a prior element, an always-already of critical discourse. Like *S/Z*, *Discourse Networks 1800/1900* approaches the text as

> an entrance into a network with a thousand entrances; to take this entrance is to aim, ultimately, not at a legal structure of norms and departures, a narrative or poetic Law, but at a perspective (of fragments, of voices from other texts, other codes), whose vanishing point is nonetheless ceaselessly pushed back, mysteriously opened: each (single) text is the very theory (and not the mere example) of this vanishing, of this difference which indefinitely returns, insubmissive. (12)

Where Kittler departs from Barthes, however, is that he does not fastidiously catalogue an entire text (in Barthes's case, the novelette *Sarasine*) in order to demonstrate that it is composed of a handful of interwoven discourses (Barthes's 'codes'). Instead, Kittler draws on a single scene as an inlet into a network of discourses that circulate through the text. In Barthesian terms, Kittler is like those 'Buddhists whose ascetic practices enable them to see a whole landscape in a bean' (Barthes 1974: 3). A single scene from Faust, for example, 'is the very theory' of discourse networks. The text is not something to critique or comment on, but a generator of theories.

Kittler, then, does not write about Faust or about Goethe; he writes *with* Goethe, just as he writes *with* Foucault, Lacan, and Derrida. This tendency of Kittler to write *with* several theorists at once is, according to David Wellberry, an innovation in scholarly method:

> Kittler's work cannot be classified as Derridean, Foucauldian, or Lacanian; rather, it grounds itself on what might be termed the joint achievement of the three. Perhaps this is the major methodological innovation of Kittler's book. By

eliciting from the divergent elaborations of post-structuralist thought a collective epistemological apparatus, Kittler establishes a positive research program
for a post-hermeneutic criticism. (1990: xi)

It is by means of this *writing with* that Kittler departs from the discourse of
the Republic of Scholars.

The Republic of Scholars

In order to fully understand why this *writing with* is an innovative form of
writing, it is necessary to take a closer look at the Republic of Scholars, from
whose practice it deviates. As I have already indicated, following David
Wellbery, the meaning of 'Republic of Scholars' is not stable; it varies
according to specific nationalities and academic traditions. Rather than providing a definition or comprehensive genealogy of the form of the Republic
that I wish to address here, I prefer, like Kittler, to identify its traces. After
all, I am writing under the aegis of electracy (elec-trace-y).[8] A genealogy of
the Republic that I wish to discuss here has already been attempted by Walter Ong, and more recently by Jay Bolter, both of whom share an interdisciplinary interest in classical culture and new media. This Republic of Scholars
extends at least as far back as Peter Ramus, the father of scholarly method,
and its presence can be traced in many places ever since: in the simultaneous
emergence of print technology and scholarly method; in Enlightenment
rationality; in the formation of a literary 'canon'; and, finally, in the spread of
Kantian critique, which is still being practised in the various mutations of
hermeneutic, textual scholarship that is prevalent in the humanities today.
This Republic of Scholars, with its faith in transparent language, scientific
proof, and the text-based, linear, sequential essay, provides the methodology
and discourse for all who wish to maintain affiliation within the academic
apparatus.

   The relatively new discipline of film studies provides a useful case study in
demonstrating the ubiquity of the discourse of the Republic of Scholars in the
academy. In no other field of research, it would seem, has there been such a
strong impetus for scholars to break the circuit of conventional scholarly discourse. No other field (except perhaps the emergent field of digital media
studies) has so fully embraced the textual theories of Derrida, Barthes et al.,
primarily as a means of understanding experimental film, and of exposing
the ideological structures of mass media. Still, as Robert Ray has shown in *The
Avant-Garde Finds Andy Hardy*, film studies seems to produce nothing but
hermeneutic essays presented in a conventional format, and built upon arguments that have now become doxa. In the past three decades, film studies,
Ray asserts, has 'constructed an enormously powerful theoretical machine
for exposing the ideological abuse hidden by the apparently natural stories

and images of popular culture. That machine, however, now runs on automatic pilot, producing predictable essays and books on individual cases' (1995: 7). We might say that the practitioners – all essayists – of film studies have been subscribing to a different sort of 'magic bean' approach to theory. That is, once they see a landscape in a bean (a film filtered through this or that 'bean theory'), they insist on recycling this process, testing its magical decoding powers on any other landscape that looks as if it might be written on a bean. This is the tale of a potentially radical form of discourse trapped in the reductive, discursive loop of the Republic of Scholars.

What, then, is the alternative to this recycling of critical doxa, this 'endless circulation' which simply 'heaves words around'? How do we break a circuit so powerfully charged that it can cause a discipline 'whose beginnings coincided with the flowering of structuralist, semiotic, ideological, psychoanalytic, and feminist theory' to evolve 'into another professional speciality (like Romanticism or Eighteenth-Century Poetry), with all the routinized procedures of any academic field' (Ray 1995: 5)? The answer, according to Ray, lies in 'experimenting with the *forms* of criticism, which until now has worked almost entirely with one kind of rhetoric,' that is, the rhetoric of the Republic of Scholars (9, emphasis added). Citing Michael Taussig, Ray suggests that 'what is at stake with such questions is "the issue of graphicness," a quality generally disdained by materialist critics who associate it with the enemies – commerce and mystification' (9). It is this yearning for graphicness that directs Ray to the avant-garde arts in search of exemplars. To Ray, the avant-garde is 'a field of experimental work waiting to be used (in the same way that pure science's exotica becomes another generation's technology)' (10).

Rather than write with Goethe, then, or with Foucault, as Kittler has done, one might try writing with Max Ernst, with Salvador Dali, or perhaps even with Stephen Gibb, as was attempted at the beginning of this chapter. Where *E-Crit* departs from *Discourse Networks 1800/1900* is in the yearning for a more explicit graphicness in academic discourse, a yearning shared by Michael Taussig and Robert Ray. If indeed we are in the thralls of a hypervisual, picture-oriented, digital age, then a scholarly discourse suitable to such an age must accept not only poststructuralism as prior knowledge, but also the fact that technologies of representation have induced a pictorial turn in our culture, subsequently placing us on the threshold of a new subjectivation that we are still in the process of understanding. Before we can take this pictorial turn as prior knowledge, however, it is of course necessary to provide some evidence of its existence.

Picture Theory[9]

Since, once again, I am engaging in an activity of tracing, or tracking down c(l)ues, in order to make linkages within the archives of a given field of information (rather than attempting to compile a taxonomy or history of the entire field), and since I am indeed dealing with the question of a pictorial turn, it might be useful to present this interrogation of picture theory in the form of a picture or graph rather than that of an essay. Of course, unwieldy graphical representation would never make its way through the cogs of the current academic apparatus except in very rare cases, such as Katherine Hayles's *Writing Machines* or Marshall McLuhan's *The Medium Is the Massage*.[10] But those who lack such academic notoriety (let alone the generous financial backing of a lucrative press) should not shrink from at least conjecturing about graphic strategies. That being said, imagine the various intersections, linkages, and lines of flight incited by the following plotting of points on a graph: from Jonathan Crary's historical evaluation of 'Scopic Regimes' to W.J.T. Mitchell's identification of a 'pictorial turn'; from E.H. Gombrich's theory of the 'mental set' to Rosalind Kraus's 'optical unconscious.' This would not be the type of graph that, in Greimasian fashion, sets up and explodes a series of binary oppositions. The graph would have to represent several contiguous points as well, and it would certainly have to be diachronic in nature. Robert Ray's 'cinematic criticism,' for example, would probably have to line up with Barthes's rendering of the 'filmic'; while the latter's investigation of the 'third meaning' might intersect at a thousand points with Gregory Ulmer's 'Chorography.' And what would we do with Derrida? Perhaps *The Truth in Painting* could serve as a frame for the graph, surround the entire structure, set itself against or beside (*contre*) all the other texts as a form of contraband in itself. Or Derrida himself might act as a *passe-partout*, weaving his way in and out of the graph, leaving traces, but no origin. Then, again, a single scene or image from *The Truth in Painting* could serve as the rectangular grid upon which all the other texts could be plotted like so many intersecting sets of coordinates; in such a case, all texts would criss-cross endlessly through a single background text – a background that is foregrounded, so to speak.

This speculative imaging, I'm sure you will agree, is far too complex for the written word, and provides a regrettable instance of the failure of language. As Rosalind Krauss observes in *The Optical Unconscious*, in the case of a graph, 'it's both less tiresome and clearer just to show it' (13). But show what? There is no print-based artefact so accommodating that it could represent the complex network of possibilities posed by the intersection of the various texts that I wish to gather here under the aegis of picture theory. Derrida's 'double-bind' model, as practised in *Glas*, can only accommodate two bands, two sets of coordinates; the semiotic square, four. Is this the same sort of representational conundrum that perplexed Walter Benjamin, causing him to relegate his *Passagen-Werk* to the confines of a suitcase while he searched fruitlessly – in the iron and glass architecture of the Paris Arcades – for a framework that would support the convolutions of his extensive project? Evidently another, more accommodating model is required to present the given network of texts in a way that does not, in Benjamin's words, 'come at the cost of graphicness (*Anschaulichkeit*)' (1989: N2, 6); a model capable of accommodating the structural and material remainders of the preceding chapter.

Perhaps a more accessible way to visualize such a model is to imagine the non-linear, graphic-rich environment of the Web. Would it complicate things to suggest that, if this essay were a hypertext, its explanation of picture theory would span various nodes?[11] It might begin with a text bite from Ernst Gombrich, complete with an extensive gallery of JPEG images, an archive documenting a culture assailed by visual stimuli:

> **gombrich.html**. Never before has there been an age like ours when the visual image was so cheap in every sense of the word. We are surrounded and assailed by posters and advertisements, by comics and magazine illustrations. We see aspects of reality represented on the television screen and in the movies, on postage stamps and on food packages. Painting is taught at school and practiced at home as therapy and as a pastime, and many a modest amateur has mastered tricks that would have looked like sheer magic to Giotto. Perhaps even the crude colored renderings we find on a box of breakfast cereal would have made Giotto's contemporaries gasp. I do not know if there are people who conclude from this that the box is superior to a Giotto. I am not one of them. But I think that the victory and vulgarization of representational skills create a problem for both the historian and the critic. (1969: 8)

And this node, in turn, might be linked to another, less lengthy explanation of the pictorial turn provided by W.J.T. Mitchell:

> **mitchell.html**. For anyone who is skeptical about the need for/to picture theory, I simply ask them to reflect on the commonplace notion that we live in a culture of images, a society of the spectacle, a world of semblances and simulacra. We are surrounded by pictures; we have an abundance of theories about them, but it doesn't seem to do us any good. (1994: 5)

For an exemplary scene of this 'culture of images,' the viewers might click their way to a MPEG video (farewell.mpg) of the 'short-subject film' in which Ronald and Nancy Reagan board a Marine helicopter and are swept away in a noisy whirl of journalists, cameras, and security people. This hypericonic video, or 'Reagan's Farewell' as Jerome McGann has baptized it, could be linked to McGann's commentary on the structure of such a 'text':

> **mcgann.html**. In a scene where speaking and communicating with words appear to be of central importance, language has been structurally translated into visual and oral tokens – as image, or as non-linguistic sound. Complex

meanings are being communicated here, but the verbal discourse – what Ezra Pound called 'logopoeia' – functions principally along nonverbal lines. To understand this text it is not necessary actually to hear anything said by Reagan or anything by the reporters. (1991: 14)

Of course, this juxtaposition of fragments would seem more appropriate within the framework of a hypertext, but the Republic of Scholars would not easily submit to an unconventional 'essay' that relies on non-linear linkage and copious graphics (this is precisely what my dissertation committee told me). And so I must satisfy myself with the printed rendition above, which, I hope, provides a fairly good sampling of what might be called picture theory.

The fact that we live in a 'visual culture,' as many critics, including those above, complacently observed at the end of the twentieth century, is not an astounding news item; our culture has been primarily 'visual' for several centuries. As Martin Jay reminds us in his 'Scopic Regimes of Modernity,' 'Beginning with the Renaissance and the scientific revolution, modernity has been normally considered resolutely ocularcentric. The invention of printing, according to the familiar argument of McLuhan and Ong, reinforced the privileging of the visual abetted by such inventions as the telescope and the microscope' (1988: 3). Jay's central concern in this essay is not so much that the moderns were primarily visual, but that various types, or 'regimes,' of visuality compose a network of discourses on visuality – from Cartesian perspectivism to baroque delirium – which circulate freely throughout the modern era. It is the spirit of the baroque regime, Jay notes, the ocular madness definitive of the baroque, which seems to reign supreme in postmodern culture.[12] This baroqueness is heightened to an unprecedented degree by electronic technologies of representation and reproduction, which insure that every facet of daily life is saturated with pictures. Western culture as it stands today is often viewed as a veritable ocular orgy, a culture that invented the term 'eye candy,' a culture that, in the terms of W.J.T. Mitchell, has indeed undergone the 'pictorial turn.'

We must draw a distinction, then, between a visual or ocularcentric culture and a culture dominated by images, a *pictorial culture*, so to speak. It is the image-saturation of our society that inspired Barthes's filmic criticism; provoked E.H. Gombrich to question 'what is actually involved in the process of image making and image reading' (1969: 25); and incited Mitchell to (seek out a) picture theory. Mitchell goes so far as to suggest that this pictorial turn is responsible for some of the most groundbreaking philosophical inquiries of the twentieth century:

In Europe one might identify it [the pictorial turn] with phenomenology's inquiry into imagination and visual experience; or with Derrida's 'grammatology,' which de-centers the 'phonocentric' model of language by shifting attention to the visible material traces of writing; or with the Frankfurt School's investigations of modernity, mass culture, and visual media; or with Michel Foucault's insistence on a history and theory of power/knowledge that exposes the rift between the discursive and the 'visible,' the seeable and the sayable, as the crucial fault-line in 'scopic regimes.' (1994: 12)

These theoretical exemplars are essential in the invention of a new mode of academic discourse. But as I have already argued, the theorists who have followed in their footsteps have failed to fully acknowledge and build upon the experimental form, the graphicness, that characterized their methods.

In addition to this, the idea of claiming that a social/psychological/cognitive phenomenon such as the 'pictorial turn' is at the root of deconstruction would be uncharacteristic of contemporary critical theory, which eschews any method that focuses on 'origins.' But I would argue that it is just this cognitive/psychological approach that is lacking today, in a culture whose visual field is incessantly bombarded by media images. In response to this lapse within critical theory, art theorist Johanna Drucker turns to Julia Kristeva and Fredric Jameson for a poststructuralist theory of visuality. In *The Visible Word*, Drucker notes that 'Jameson, writing in relation to his work in *The Political Unconscious*, saw the necessity for linking ideological production to a motivated, psychoanalytically complex subject as a means of explaining the efficacy of ideological form' (40). This emphasis on subject positioning, I would argue, is key to the production of new modes of scholarly discourse.

Among the many theoretical investigations of contemporary visuality, E.H. Gombrich's *Art and Illusion*, a classic psycho-historical study of the fine arts, is perhaps the most convincing attempt to demonstrate the intricate interdependence of the eye and the field of vision. Not only is perspective a visual illusion according to Gombrich, but it is a culturally determined effect that relies upon the fact that the brain, indeed, is not separate from the world it contemplates. Perspective, according to Gombrich, 'creates its most compelling illusion where it can rely on certain ingrained expectations and assumptions on the part of the beholder. The Baroque decorator's illusion of painted ceilings or architecture works so well because these paintings represent what might, after all, be real' (261). Gombrich's crucial theoretical contribution to this study is the 'mental set,' a subjective 'horizon of expectation' (60) that guides an individual's optical impressions. Vision, in Gombrich's model, is a form of projection, and each individual possesses mental schemata against which s/he attempts to match the shapes in her/his field of vision. Thus, that which 'we call "reading" an image,' Gombrich suggests, 'may perhaps be better described as testing it for its potentialities' (227).

In a postmodern world of video art lessons and virtual reality 'tours' of paintings (an experience that seems almost pornographic), the seeing individual must rely continuously on the 'mental set' in order to make sense of the pictorial spectacle that unfolds daily before him. To explain the working of the mental set, Gombrich uses the example of modern poster artists, who often 'rely on our expectation of the normal letter form to give us the impression of letters or words arranged in depth or coming toward us with aggressive force' (261). Although we may wish to modernize this example by pointing instead to the digital animations found on Web-page banner ads, the point remains the same: 'it is an effect which would be lost on someone who did not know the conventions of lettering' (261).

The selection of advertising media as an example is not entirely arbitrary here, for in the field of advertising the ability to predict or recognize and play (prey) upon the 'mental sets' of an unwitting audience is the professional *raison d'être*. The existence of culturally determined mental sets provides advertisers with a means of creating ads that will target a specific audience and insure a predictable emotional response. For example, the use of Martin Luther King's 'I have a dream' speech allowed a technology company to graft emotions related to social progress into a message about technological progress. But the most successful advertising strategies are able to insert their own images into the audience's mental set. The Nike symbol, primordial archetype of everything athletic, is a case in point – an exercise in the corporate manipulation of human pattern recognition.

There are, however, certain methods of classification within 'the filing systems of our mind' (Gombrich 1969: 105) that are not culturally determined, but that are entirely personal and subjective, the result of an individual's psychic experience.[13] These mental images may not even be recognized by the individual herself, although they may have radical effects on the way she organizes visual stimuli. I will investigate such images in greater detail in a later chapter. For the moment, I will simply suggest that Gombrich's claim that human perception relies upon 'projection,' or on our ability to reference 'mental sets' that are culturally, physiologically, and personally determined, marks an important moment in the history of picture theory. Gombrich's research helps point the way to a scholarly discourse suitable to a culture that is constantly subjected to pictorial manipulations, a culture in which individuals are incessantly called upon to 'project' themselves into media images.

Jerome McGann seems to pick up on Gombrich's notion of projection in his seminal structuralist essay 'How to Read a Book.' In this essay, McGann identifies three operations, or *modes of reading*, involved in any act of reading: the linear, which decodes the logos of the text; the spatial, which involves an ocular scanning of the text or image; and the radial, in which reading transcends its own 'ocular, physical bases' (26) and focuses instead on the various 'contexts that interpenetrate the scripted and physical text' (28). In the case of the radial mode of reading, McGann seems to be invoking what is more commonly known as 'intertextuality,' though taken in its broadest sense to include not only written texts, but other media and even unconscious associations or projections.

The combined work of McGann and Gombrich is essential for this study since both theorists point out, in a very straightforward manner, that the process of reading text or pictures involves various physical and mental operations, some of which the reader may not always be aware. In order to withstand the image bombardment being deployed in the current mediascape, readers and viewers must possess a means of filtration that will allow them to consciously organize visual information and arrange it into manageable patterns. But in order to develop such an apparatus, it seems that a reader must dismiss the notion of transparent communication, and accept the impossibility of a universal perspective, or of 'a purely responsive act of reading – an act which will decode the transmission in precisely the way that the sender desires' (McGann 1991: 37). Once this understanding has been achieved, we may be able to recognize how 'the filing systems of our mind' work, and perhaps even externalize them, put them to use as a practical tool for organizing information. Those who practise new scholarly methods must be aware that 'even under the best of circumstances, messages and their senders are neither innocent nor completely reliable ... [and] readers must be prepared to defend themselves against both the errors and the perversions of those who communicate texts' (McGann 1991: 37).

Imagetext and the Sister Arts[14]

It is important to note that the picture theory exemplars above – Mitchell, Gombrich, and McGann – base much of their investigations on the interaction of image and text, a dialectical relationship that achieves its apotheosis in the ideogram. It is no coincidence that Mitchell and McGann are scholars of William Blake, the Romantic poet/painter/printmaker and master of the imagetext and ideogram. In the next chapter, I will consider Blake as an exemplar of new media discourse. First, I want to assemble a fairly cogent assemblage of theoretical exemplars, and that mix would be incomplete without Roland Barthes. As Johanna Drucker suggests in her extensive study of typographical art, much of Barthes's work, like that of the other picture theorists in this chapter, 'moves toward the inscription of a subject within the structuralist system, as an instance of the expression of the codes of language and signification' (1994: 40). Unlike those other theorists, however, Barthes may not have agreed that we live in a culture governed by the tyranny of the image. In 'Rhetoric of the Image,' Barthes asserts that even in today's world of sophisticated mass communications,

> it appears that the linguistic message is indeed present in every image: as title, caption, accompanying press article, film dialogue, comic strip balloon. Which

shows that it is not very accurate to talk of a civilization of the image – we are
still, and more than ever, a civilization of writing, writing and speech continu-
ing to be the full terms of the informational structure. (1977: 38)

Still, this bold pronouncement did not stop Barthes from investigating the
image, especially the photographic image, with painstaking, structuralist
detail. In 'The Photographic Message,' Barthes asks: 'How do we read a photograph? What do we perceive? In what order, according to what progression?' (1977: 28). He answers his own question, not by invoking mental sets or
modes of reading, but by describing the 'denoted' and 'connoted' messages of
an image. The denoted message, according to Barthes, designates the mimetic
property of the image, the image as analogon to reality. The 'connoted' message is subtler, however, for it implies 'the manner in which the society to a
certain extent communicates what it thinks of it [the image]' (1977: 17).

At this point, it may seem that Barthes's theory of connotation is directly in
line with theories of visualization proposed by Gombrich and McGann. But
the correlation is not so simple. Since they all share a similar concept of visuality, we could propose that Barthes, McGann, and Gombrich are all spokes-
men for a single postmodern scopic regime. We might compare Barthes's
'connoted message' to McGann's notion of the 'radial,' for both concepts
attempt to account for the various contexts interpenetrating a given image.
Even more similar are Gombrich's notions of schema and projection. In Barthes's terms, however, we immediately decode an image according to a
socially constructed 'stock of signs,' the perceptual schemata unique to a
given culture (1977: 21). 'There is no perception,' Barthes argues, following
the structuralist theories of Piaget, 'without immediate categorization' (1977:
28). However, unlike Gombrich, Barthes suggests that the 'stock of signs'
available to each individual is not a schema of images, but a cultural *verbal*
reservoir. In Barthes's 'point of view, the image – grasped immediately by an
inner metalanguage, language itself – in actual fact has no denoted state, is
immersed for its very social existence in at least an initial layer of connotation,
that of the categories of language' (1977: 28). For Barthes, then, the classification system of the mind is merely a culturally determined, linguistic apparatus, and hence there is no sense talking about subjective mental sets
composed of distinct images, shapes, or patterns. We are destined to remain
a linguistic and text-oriented (not pictorial) civilization.

This linguistic element of image decoding represents, for Barthes, a perplexing conundrum. It is all the more perplexing since the connotative message of an image can easily be manipulated – in the press photo, for example
– for political reasons, by simply adding a single line of text. In the case of
such manipulations, the seeming objectivity, the seeming 'denotative innocence' of a mechanically produced photograph, acts as camouflage for a
propagandist connotation. Barthes proposes, then, that Western culture, at

least within the context of his study of the press photograph, has undergone an anti-pictorial turn. The image, he insists, is always subordinated to the message imposed upon it by the written text, whether it is a caption, a headline, or some other written form. 'The text,' as Barthes observes in 'The Photographic Message,' 'constitutes a parasitic message designed to connote the image, to "quicken" it with one or more second-order signifieds ... In the relationship which now holds, it is not the image which comes to elucidate or "realize" the text, but the latter which comes to sublimate, patheticize or rationalize the image' (1977: 25).

Should we accept, then, that in the battle of signification, it is the text, alphabetic logocentrism, that carries the day, that stubbornly anchors the specific meaning of an image? Or is this true only in the very particular case of press photographs, and only in Western culture? What about other cultures and other word/picture combinations, or 'imagetexts'? Many critics and theorists have suggested that wherever images and texts share the same space, an unspoken struggle is taking place. Rosalind Krauss, for example, observes that when this contest ensues in the space of a painting, the text is clearly unseated from its privileged position. In *The Optical Unconscious*, Krauss proposes that 'as soon as writing is "framed" it becomes an image: either "writing" turned into a decorative picture of itself, as in Breton's presentations of schizophrenic production, or a projective matrix within which to see images, as Polonius saw the camel in the clouds or Leonardo the figures in the fire' (284). She notes that this representational quirk was capitalized upon by abstract impressionists such as Jackson Pollock, though it was recognized much earlier as a central 'paradox of surrealist theory' (284). She, like many critical theorists before and after her, draws on Magritte's infamous painting *La trahison des images* – a pipe, rendered with naïve simplicity, floating weightlessly above the neatly handwritten caption, 'Ceci n'est pas une pipe' – as an example of how the image in a painting can subordinate the text, render it absurd, redundant, or nonsensical. Clearly, it would seem that the visible evidence of the pipe in Magritte's painting causes the words to appear ridiculous. 'Indeed, this is a pipe,' the viewer might tell him/herself, 'the words are lying.' But the contest, as I hope to make clear, is not so easily won; nor are the rules as straightforward as Krauss portrays them to be.

The image/text question drove Michel Foucault to devote an entire study to *La trahison des images*, the caption of which serves as a title to his essay. Foucault's 'Ceci n'est pas une pipe' stresses the irreducible complexity of the image/text question, drawing on theoretical tenets proposed in *The Order of Things*. In the encounter of verbal with pictorial media, Foucault suggests, the point is not that one mode of representation is more suggestive or more powerful than the other, but that the relation between the two 'is an infinite relation' (1994: 9). Foucault argues that text and image are inextricably bound in a dialectical relationship since 'neither can be reduced to the other's terms'

(9). 'It is in vain,' Foucault argues, 'that we say what we see; what we see never resides in what we say. And it is in vain that we attempt to show, by the use of images, metaphors, or similes, what we are saying; the space where they achieve their splendour is not that deployed by our eyes but that defined by the sequential elements of syntax' (9). Foucault's argument, then, is similar to that of Barthes: it is not that images are less suggestive or powerful than words, but that the meaning of any picture or text can only be decoded in terms of the linear, sequential elements of written or verbal text. As a result, the verbal text seems to reign supreme, for it always has the last word, so to speak.

Despite the apparent ingenuousness of Magritte's painting, Foucault identifies it as a dialectical enigma, a scene of seduction into which the viewer is irresistibly drawn. A painting that might otherwise appear to be banally academic – 'My God, how simple-minded!' – is rendered complex by 'the inevitability of connecting the text to the drawing ... and the impossibility of defining a perspective that would let us say that the assertion is true, false, or contradictory' (Foucault 1982: 19, 20). Magritte's painting, which the digital pedagogy theorist Carl Raschke describes as 'a kind of "multi-media" essay on the arbitrary nature of the sign' (2003: 82), short-circuits a discursive apparatus built on the transparency of language and the discrete compartmentalization of knowledge. It presents a situation in which the very foundation of discourse begins to tremble: '... it isn't simply that the words contradict the image, and vice versa, but that the very identities of words and images, the sayable and the seeable, begin to shimmer and shift in the composition, as if the image could speak and the words were on display' (Mitchell 1994: 68).

When, years after painting *La trahison des images*, Magritte moved his pipe and caption to a blackboard mounted on an easel (see fig. 2.2), it is as if he was directly targeting the academic apparatus, taunting it with a form of discourse which it could not possibly accommodate. It is in this sense that Magritte's pipe 'is a teaching aid, a piece of classroom apparatus. Its purpose, however, is a negative lesson, an exercise in unlearning or deprogramming a set of habits which are second nature' (Mitchell 1994: 67). Magritte's pipe opens a fissure from which a new scholarly discourse might emerge.

According to W.J.T. Mitchell, Foucault's short essay demonstrates that *La trahison des images* is not only a metapicture, a *picture about pictures* that instructs us on the 'infinite relation' between image and text; it is also a hypericon that 'provides a picture of Foucault's way of writing and his whole theory of the stratification of knowledge and the relations of power in the dialectic of the visible and the sayable' (1994: 71). Foucault demonstrates that one does not have to be a painter to generate a picture theory. His essay, like Magritte's painting, short-circuits the discursive apparatus in and for which it was written, which in this case is the apparatus of the Republic of

2.2 René Magritte, *Les deux mystères*, 1966.

Scholars. Evidence of this short-circuiting lies in the fact that Foucault's body of work has created a particular dilemma in the human sciences, namely, by introducing a form of research that crosses boundaries – historical and disciplinary – and calls for a radical revision of scholarly research methodologies. Most importantly, Foucault introduces a certain graphicness into the apparatus by engaging in a form of research that is driven by the picture and the graphic scene. But Foucault is not the only scholar to engage in an unconventionally graphic form of critical discourse.

One could trace a history of anti-pictorialism in Western philosophy from Plato[15] to television-smashing neo-Luddites. Indeed, it is no surprise that text is privileged over image in the area of critical theory, which spawned out of literary study. The structure of the academic apparatus, rooted firmly in a tradition of phonocentrism and stratification of knowledge, programs the manner in which research is conducted and presented. W.J.T. Mitchell has observed that 'the corporate, departmental structure of universities reinforces the sense that verbal and visual media are to be seen as distinct, separate, and parallel spheres that convene only at some higher level of abstraction' (1994: 85). Since verbal media are the preferred vehicle of discourse in academia, then pictorial modes of representation might be considered as the *other* of scholarly discourse. It appears, then, that if the mode of representation in critical discourse is to be rendered more graphic, or if the imagetext would come to be respected as a scholarly mode of presentation, such a change would require, or at least metonymically imply, some sort of structural change in the disciplinary system of higher education. This type of sweeping structural transformation, considered briefly in the final chapter, is indeed the implied goal of this study; for any project which has internalized deconstruction must necessarily interfere 'with solid structures, "material" institutions, and not only with discourses or signifying representations' (Derrida 1987: 19). The critical/theoretical texts outlined in this chapter are committed to the interference, interruption, and deconstruction of such 'solid structures' through their graphic modes of discourse, their methods of picturing theory.

By focusing on pictures in a new mode of scholarly discourse, I am not necessarily recommending a radical revolution but, in some ways, a restoration of a holistic humanities-spurred formal experimentation in the 'sister arts.' As Johanna Drucker suggests, 'it became clear that the development of criticism in both literary criticism and visual arts had, by midcentury, come to define the realms in terms of a mutually exclusive set of assumptions' (1994: 4). Drucker notes that while art critics and historians, including Michel Seuphor, Alfred Barr, and Clement Greenberg, were trumpeting the 'autonomy of modern art,' literary critics, especially T.S. Eliot and the American New Critics, were grappling to redefine 'literature' in terms of autonomous texts whose value 'was pursued as a play of verbal terms which functioned as signs, surrogates, for a proliferating but always absent meaning – a meaning unsullied by such contingencies as authorship, intention, or historical circumstances' (1994: 4).[16] It is around this compartmentalization of art and literature that Drucker builds her study of experimental typography:

> The distinction between visual presence and semiotic/literary absence rendered experimental typography an aberration within the well-defined guidelines of high modernist criticism. Deconstructive and poststructuralist strategies have had more use of the complexities of signifying practices which do not conform to the well-ordered code of disciplinary distinctions, but the most potent aspect of typography's form – its refusal to resolve into either a visual or verbal mode – raises issues which have not, I think, been fully explored in theoretical terms. (1994: 4)

While Drucker focuses on a theoretical exploration of typography in this important study, some of her most vital work, I would argue, lies in the formal experimentations of her artist's books. These require a fuller exploration than I can provide here, but I can simply note that what I am seeking in the development of a new mode of academic discourse lies between Drucker's 'serious' theoretical work and her artist's books. This would require a more concerted effort to blur the boundaries between the visual arts and literary criticism.

In an often overlooked anthology entitled *Deconstruction and the Visual Arts*, the discourse of picture theory intersects with the contrabanding discourse of deconstruction, and the result is a series of essays dedicated to challenging the phonocentric assumptions of the Republic of Scholars. Perhaps the greatest concern of deconstruction as it turns toward the visual arts is to expose and undermine the sense-making codes that seem to dominate conventional art history and criticism – codes that strive, once again, to present a model of visual communication as transparent. As Brunette and Wills suggest in the introduction to the anthology,

> It may be this very claim of the visual arts to speak 'directly' somehow, supposedly avoiding the mediation inherent in verbal language, that is most in need of deconstruction. Even in the most abstract work of art, sense-making visual codes, sanctioned by the history of the medium, codes that tell us, for example, how to read diagonals, jagged lines, circles, and so on (and which, it could be argued, constitute a language of sorts), are always operative. (4)

Once again, the notion of coding is put forth as a primary element of visualization and of critical interpretation. In the field of visual arts, as in all academic disciplines, there is a set of institutional codes which, like the codes constructed by corporate advertisers, are instilled through education and account for an endless proliferation of doxa.

The contributors to *Deconstruction and the Visual Arts* demonstrate that it is not enough to bring these 'sense-making codes' to the surface and watch them crumble in the light of day, but that the formation of new and unexpected, even inappropriate, codes, based on contingent or obtuse meanings, must be adopted as alternative means of organizing information. Each writer in the anthology draws (the pun is essential) on the potential ideographic nature of writing in order to deconstruct the phonocentric expectations of conventional critical discourse. Jacques Derrida, whose interview with Peter Brunette sets the tone for the anthology, is, of course, at the fore of such a deconstructive undertaking. In '+R,' Derrida offers a 'picto-ideo-phonogrammatic' reading of a painting by Valerio Adami. Derrida's '+R' is more than an *analysis* of, or a *commentary* on, Adami's art; it is an attempt to transform representational practices and prejudices as we know them by invoking a more graphic critical methodology. Derrida writes *with* Adami. The encounter between deconstruction and the visual arts, then, involves more than applying the practices of deconstruction to image reading; it also implies the integration of images into the very methodology of deconstructive activity.[17] It is only through such a transgression of the institutional framework, only through such a contraband strategy, that new forms of pictorial, critical methodologies can be invented, methodologies designed to subvert the doxical at all costs.

Deconstruction and the Visual Arts attests to the fact that pictures provide an extremely fruitful ground for deconstructive activity. As Derrida suggests, 'It is within a certain experience of spacing, of space, that resistance to philosophical authority can be produced. In other words, resistance to logocentrism has a better chance of appearing in these types [that is, graphic types] of art' (in Brunette and Wills 1994: 10). The obvious example of this resistance, as I have already suggested, is in the work of the avant-garde, where artists ply their trade in the hope of altering not only various institutional frameworks, but human perception in general.[18] The goal of surrealism, for example, spearheaded by André Breton, was to effect a transformation of everyday life through the means of another methodological contraband: the importation of psychoanalytic theory into fine art.[19]

In *The Optical Unconscious*, Rosalind Krauss explores the work of a variety of avant-garde artists, from Max Ernst to Jackson Pollock, in the attempt to designate what might be called an alternative scopic regime. In this painstaking research experiment, Krauss demonstrates how the avant-garde, through its persistent attempts to represent the unconscious drives and desires behind human perception, disrupted and still haunts modern art and the institutions that have come to define it. *The Optical Unconscious* is not only an indispensable tool for the study of modernism and the avant-garde, but, more importantly, for the study and perhaps transformation of theory and criticism as they are generally practised today. Krauss's work is characterized by an innovative and unconventional graphicness that marks a change in the way critical theory can be performed and presented. Like Katherine Hayles in *Writing Machines*, Krauss's close attention to the materiality of her subject results in the invention of a new mode of discourse composed of imagetexts.

Certainly, the graphical richness of *The Optical Unconscious* qualifies it as an art aficionado's fetish item, a veritable archive of avant-garde reproductions. But what makes the book truly valuable is that it possesses a certain theoretical pictorialism, a certain critical iconicity even, that sets it apart from other studies in the visual arts. This pictorialism is evidenced not only in Krauss's persistent reliance on graphs and other visual schemata, but in the images she selects to illustrate her points, some of which seem to act independently of the text. More specifically, *The Optical Unconscious* is held together by a network of hypericons: images that encapsulate the theories of knowledge that are under examination in the book.

Since this facet of Krauss's work would require the attention of an entire study in order to be explained sufficiently, I have been forced to resign

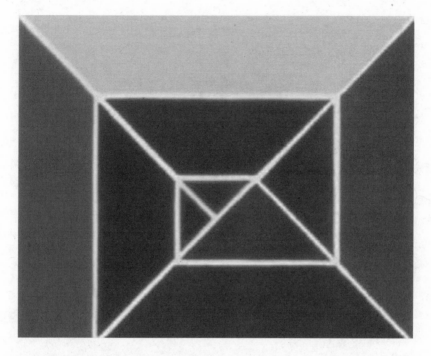

2.3 Frank Stella, *Hyena Stomp* (detail), 1962.

myself to a single example. At the beginning of each chapter of *The Optical Unconscious*, we find an icon – a detail from a painting, drawing, or photograph – that serves as the title. The title of each chapter, then, is represented by a pictorial *mise en abyme*,[20] a conceptually – and ideologically – loaded image that captures the central argument of each chapter. The title of chapter 1, for example, a chapter concerning the slippage between figure and ground prevalent in modern art, is a detail from Frank Stella's painting *Hyena Stomp* (fig. 2.3). Although Krauss does not comment on this pictorial chapter title, it is apparent that this image serves as a hypericon: a compact, painterly representation of her argument. In this case, she is arguing that the semiotic square, as employed by Greimas and the Klein group, is an oversimplified model that propagates a false effect of transparency or objectivity. One might compare the perfect conceptual symmetry of the semiotic grid with Stella's *Louisiana Lottery Company* (fig. 2.4), the very first painting reproduced in the chapter. Although Krauss does not explicitly compare the semiotic square and Stella's series of concentric rectangles, the similarity is difficult to ignore – the painting speaks for itself.

2.4 Frank Stella, *Louisiana Lottery Company,* 1962.

As Krauss's argument progresses, the semiotic square, with its tidy binary juxtapositions, is rejected for Lacan's L-Schema, a more complex graph in which 'the relationships are in permanent circulation, continuous flow. Their dynamic is productive, producing repetition, and the circuit interrupts the perfect symmetry of the graph' (24). It is appropriate that from the beginning to the end of the chapter we should progress from the simple and symmetrical *Louisiana Lottery Company* to Stella's *Hyena Stomp*, a trompe l'oeil in which an apparent series of concentric squares turns out to yield a more complex pattern – that of a spiral, a rectangular vortex. The suggestive detail from this painting placed at the beginning of the chapter is a hypericon, then, a graphic representation of what Krauss identifies as the central problem of *The Optical Unconscious*: 'to show that the depths are there, to show

2.5 Frank Stella, *Hyena Stomp*, 1962.

that the graph's transparency is only seeming; that it masks what is beneath it, or to use a stronger term, *represses* it' (27, Krauss's emphasis). By drawing on the work of the avant-garde, Krauss invents a remarkably graphic decon- structive methodology. The Stella icon that appears at the beginning of the chapter is at once an archetype of avant-garde methodology, a heuristic, mnemonic device,[21] and a deconstructive tool.

Remediating Theory

I would argue that Krauss's iconic methodology would be easily adaptable to an electronic environment, where the 'icon' appears as frequently as the writ- ten word and imagetexts are the most frequent mode of representation. In

Writing Space, a seminal historical overview of writerly spaces of representation from papyrus to the computer terminal, Jay Bolter notes that electronic writing presents us with the most complex form of visual communication since the illuminated manuscript. 'Reading the complex electronic page,' Bolter explains,

> demands an attention to text, image, and their relationships. Readers must move back and forth from the linear presentation of verbal text to the two-dimensional field of electronic picture writing. They can read the alphabetic signs in the conventional way, but they must also parse diagrams, illustrations, windows, and icons. Electronic readers therefore shuttle between two modes of reading, or rather they learn to read in a way that combines verbal and picture reading. Their reading includes activating signs by typing and moving the cursor and then making symbolic sense of the motions that their movements produce. (71)

The protean nature of the computer interface seems to be an ideal way of accommodating a pictorial, deconstructive discourse such as that of Krauss. Certainly, this would be the claim of Bolter, who, in *Writing Space*, argues that hypertext confirms, and gives a visible structure to, deconstructive textual theories that are otherwise difficult to represent or comprehend.

Of course, deconstructive activity is not medium-specific; but the electronic 'writing space' provides a more apt way of representing the concepts of deconstruction, and is also a practical tool for conducting transgressive image/text experiments. Electronic media, then, can be essential in delivering a new mode of scholarly discourse, 'an alternative rhetoric, a way out of the traditional prison of sequential exposition and logical argument' (Ray 1995: 82). In *Heuretics*, Gregory Ulmer suggests that electronic media might be used to invent a 'hyperrhetoric,' a rhetoric 'that replaces the logic governing argumentative writing with associational networks' (18). It is not just a matter of using electronic media to visually represent certain tenets – 'death of the author,' 'readerly vs. writerly texts,' 'intertextuality,' etc. – of poststructural theory. This has already been done. My approach here is to put poststructuralism to work as the software required for inventing new theories, new modes of discourse, new poetics capable of short-circuiting the discourse of the Republic of Scholars.

The electronic tools only account for a portion of the new apparatus. In truth, we do not know exactly how to use these tools in a way that will adequately serve our need of inventing a new discourse. There are no Microsoft software bundles that tell us how to invent a new scholarly methodology. One alternative might be to design our own (non-electronic) software, or our own discursive approaches based on models provided by methodological inventors of discourse in our cultural history, including those I have presented in this chapter. In *The Language of New Media*, Lev Manovich suggests that 'by looking at the history of visual culture and media, in particular, cinema, we can find many strategies and techniques relevant to new media design. Put differently, to develop a new aesthetics of new media, we should pay as much attention to cultural history as to the computer's unique new possibilities to generate, organize, manipulate, and distribute data' (314). But it is not necessary to limit the search for exemplars to cinema. While Ray, Ulmer, Krauss, and others appropriately turn to twentieth-century avant-garde art for a repertoire of exemplars in the formation of a new 'poetics,' examples of a more graphic, 'alternative rhetoric' existed long before André Breton composed *Nadja*. The Romantic poet and artist William Blake, for example, was producing his own experimental poetics in the late eighteenth and early nineteenth centuries, drawing on the subversive power of image-texts and conveying his ideology through a self-devised form of 'new media,' an 'infernal method' of printing. I wonder what Blake would have done if his desktop was equipped not with burins, acids, and copper plates, but with a Mac (or would Blake prefer a PC?), Photoshop, Netscape, and Flash?[22] Such questions are nonsensical, of course, but they are not outside the boundaries of this study.

What, then, are we to do with the (admittedly incomplete) list of ingredients assembled in this chapter? Rather than dwell eternally on what I don't know – the immobilizing flaw of all scholars – perhaps I should move forward (if that is, indeed, the direction), take stock of what I *do* know, and run the machine through a series of controlled experiments. What I do know is that the mode of discourse that I am trying to invent here is geared toward interrupting the circuit of the Republic of Scholars. I know that similar interruptions have been successful in the avant-garde arts. I know that the closest thing to such an interruption in the field of criticism occurs through post-structural theory and models of discursivity built on the network paradigm. And finally, I understand that since this discourse is created in and for a culture that is both computer- and picture-oriented, then it must make full use of these representational tools. In *After Theory*, Terry Eagleton suggests that 'writers like Barthes, Foucault, Kristeva and Derrida were really late modernist artists who had taken to philosophy rather than to sculpture or the novel' (65). These theorists were essentially 'well informed dilettantes' at a time when the term 'cultural theorist' took over for the label of 'the intellectual.' What would it take to restore this aesthetically informed dissidence to scholarship in a post-theory, information age when cultural theory has become an institutionalized specialization? In a later chapter, I will respond to this by suggesting that 'digital dilettantism,' flying in the face of academic compartmentalization and specialization, might be an effective strategy. But first, in response to Eagleton's suggestion that the inventors of 'high theory' were essentially artists, I turn in the next chapter from theoretical exemplars to an artistic exemplar, William Blake, while simultaneously practising the poetics of *hypericonomy*, as outlined in the first chapter.

3. THE HYPERICONIC DE-VISE: Peter Ramus Meets William Blake

Things are immensely numerous, and their various properties and differences from one another are likewise immensely numerous. Hence it is that all the things which go with each and every individual thing, or which fail to go with it, cannot possibly be embraced by any utterance or by the human mind ... Thus, greatly gifted men have cut out from this profuse variety of things these common headings (capita), such as substance, cause, result, and others which we shall treat of, so that when we set ourselves to thinking about some certain thing, following these headings, we may go immediately through the whole nature and parts of the thing in question.
  – Rudolph Agricola, *De inventione dialectica* (1479), trans. in Walter J. Ong,
    Ramus, Method, and the Decay of Dialogue, 117–18

Books for Little Boys: Thomas Murner and Peter Ramus

The epigraph above contains the seeds of a tree known as Ramism. To describe Ramism as a 'tree'[1] is more than just a coy metaphor, for the image of the tree seems to underlie almost all that we know about Ramism. When Agricola speaks of *cutting out* headings from a 'profuse variety of things,' he is drawing on an arboreal metaphorical tradition whose roots go as far down as Greek philosophy. In the Renaissance literary and philosophical tradition, the term *silva*, Latin for woods or forest, was often associated with disorder and confusion, a profusion of 'things' which one had to 'cut out' or cut through in order to arrive at a destination. Hence we have texts such as Ben Jonson's *Timber* and *The Underwood*,[2] and Francis Bacon's *Sylva Sylvarum* (*A Forest of Forests*), a hodgepodge of commentary on natural history. Of course, among the logicians and pedagogues of the late Middle Ages and Renaissance, there was less interest in producing forests of information than in cutting through such forests, and organizing them in a manner that could be stored and recalled on demand. This drive toward classification based on the

3.1 Antique book press.

placing of information within an organized space – not in a forest, then, but in the branches of a tree – is what we have come to call topical logic, or 'place-logic,' a concept that many literary theorists before me, such as Walter J. Ong, have covered in detail while providing a scholarly history of print culture.

What if I were writing a history of print culture, not for scholars, but for little boys? I might start by describing the scene of Peter Ramus's decapitation. Ramus, the patriarch of print-centric scholarly method, was murdered during the St Bartholomew's Day Massacre on 26 August 1572. To be precise, he was decapitated, thrown out a window, and cast into the Seine, an act that, in Gregory Ulmer's foreboding words, 'suggests some relationship between discourses on method and murder' (1994: 18). While the parents of little boys might object to this introduction as a scheming use of violence to add spice to an otherwise boring lesson, I would argue that the scene of Ramus's decapitation can act as a suitably grotesque mnemonic device, a hypericonic vehicle that can carry the little boys through an entire lesson on the print apparatus, and help them remember it once they are done. Of course, that response would have to be followed by an explanation of *hypericon*, *mnemonic*, *apparatus*, and their interrelationships. I would also have to explain the rationale for choosing a particularly monstrous scene. My goal is to pursue such an explanation here (even though I have no intention of writing a book for little boys) by introducing a post-Ramist scholarly method that I have come to call *hypericonomy*.

As the epigraph above demonstrates, our 'information society' is not the first to feel overwhelmed by an onslaught of information, nor is it the first to draw on 'new media' as a means of organizing that information. Agricola's *De inventione dialectica* (1479) responds to information overload by providing a discourse on method that instructs readers in the ways of logical organization. Agricola's method, a form of pre-Renaissance new media, involves placing 'things' under their proper headings, and distributing them in an external writing space rather than containing them entirely in memory. Agricola and his methodological predecessors succeeded in moving the mnemonic place-logic of classical orators (recalling stories or arguments by arranging them within an internalized space) into an external writing space, an achievement that is entirely taken for granted in our age of late print. When Jay Bolter, for example, uses the term 'writing space' to indicate 'the physical and visual field defined by a particular technology of writing' (1991: 11), he is speaking within a Ramist tradition that views technologies of writing as technologies of containment or storage. 'The pre-Agricolan mind,' Ong suggests, 'had preferred to think of books as saying something, of sentences as expressing something, and of words and ideas as "containing" nothing at all but rather as signifying or making signs for something. After Agricola the notion of content can serve for and level out all these diversified modes of conceptualization' (1958: 121). Eventually, the *topos* (place) of *topical logic* lost its literal sense, leaving us with the more abstract word *topic*, which is the darling of composition instructors. As Walter Ong has argued, the dialectical method of Agricola and, even more so, that of Peter Ramus a century later 'was to prove itself unexpectedly congenial to printing techniques' (1958: 97). These techniques contained thoughts within the pages of a book and, I will add, encouraged the practice of sitting immobile while studying. From the perspective of little boys, could there be a worse fate?

While it may seem strange to dwell on little boys as I have done here, I am simply alluding to a reality in the phallogocentric history of the print apparatus: the methods of Agricola and Ramus were designed specifically for young boys. As Ong explains in *Ramus, Method, and the Decay of Dialogue*,

> In Ramus' day and earlier, the student might begin all his studies at the university, attaching himself to a master about the age of seven, as Ramus himself explains. The boy studied grammar until the age of ten or twelve, rhetoric from twelve to fourteen, philosophy at about fifteen or earlier ... The student became a master of arts – which meant, in principle, that he had completed his studies in grammar, rhetoric, and *all* philosophy, for there were only medicine, law, or theology after this – at the age of eighteen except at Paris, where statutes forbade anyone to act as master before twenty. (136)

The gender and youthfulness of MA students during the Renaissance may go a long way in explaining the methodologies and pedagogical materials used by their instructors. Consider, for example, a passage from Thomas Wilson's *The Rule of Reason* (1553), the first book on logic to appear in English:

> He that will take profeicte in this parte of logique, must bee like a hunter, and learne by labour to knowe the boroughes. For these places bee nothing elles, but covertes or boroughes, wherein if any one search diligently, he maie finde game at pleasure. And although perhappes one place faile him, yet shal he finde a dousen other places, to accoumplishe his purpose. Therefore if any one will dooe good in this kinde, he must goe from place to place, and by searching every borough he shal have his purpose undoubtedly in moste part of them, if not in al. (Quoted in Ong 1958: 120)

Wilson's sly attempt to engage students in a virtual foxhunt may well be one of the very first samples of an educational 'video game,' a concept that I will explore briefly in the next chapter.

Of course, there are more appropriate precedents to the tradition of teaching with visual aids, such as Thomas Murner's *Chartiludium logice* or logical card game (1509). Murner provides young students with a woodcut set of iconic flashcards representing the elements of logical discourse. *Enunciation* is represented by a little bell, *predicament* by a fish, *prolepsis* by a grasshopper,

2 predicabile

3.2 Mnemonic figure from Thomas Murner's *Logical Card Game*, 1509.

and so on. Ong sees the production of Murner's logical card game as a result of the changing (Copernican) attitudes toward space in the Renaissance. The game also seems to emerge from the moralistic emblem-book tradition of the early print era. What's important here is that these texts document a shift from strictly mnemonic, internalized practices to methodologies that are reliant upon the external spatialization of thought. What contemporary readers might consider the cartoonish visual quality of these materials has less to do with the age of students than it does with the pervasive iconicity that characterized pre-print texts and the mnemonic mode of discourse that spawned them. Murner's cards should not be seen as an effort to pander to the sensibilities of little boys (I'll leave that to the creators of educational video games), but as a calculated, though short-lived, attempt to translate a pictorial logic from the virtual space of memory to the hard, material space of a textbook. What makes Murner's work short-lived is that it met its greatest foe in Peter Ramus, whose logical method could be applied not only to pedagogy, but also to the growing print materiality of books.

There was no place in Ramus's logical method for mnemonic icons in any form, whether they be externalized or internalized. In fact, Ramus dismissed the works of Aristotle and Cicero for their reliance upon randomly selected mnemonic devices, which he considered as 'external and fictitious signs and representations' (Ong 1958: 194). Although many pre-Ramist thinkers may have conceived of the notion of *efficiency* and applied it to logical argumentation, Ramus was, perhaps, the first logician to use the term 'method' deliberately. For Ramus, method referred specifically to the 'orderly pedagogical presentation of any subject by reputedly scientific descent from "general principles" to "specials" by means of definition and bipartite division' (Ong 1958: 30). *Arbitrary* mnemonic devices had to be discarded from Ramus's

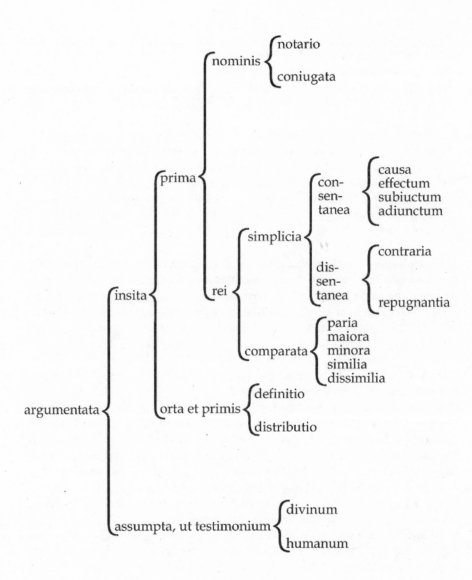

3.3 Omer Talon, table of dichotomies: from *Training in Dialectic*, 1547.

tables of dichotomies, which he claimed were based on 'the order found within things themselves,' and thus were to be considered as 'the truest possible representations' of reality (Ong 1958: 194). According to Ong, Ramus was simply responding to the need of universities to corporatize knowledge delivery:

> ... in the university, the teacher was also part of a corporation which was uncalculatingly but relentlessly reducing the personalist, dialoguing element in knowledge to a minimum in favor of an element which made knowledge something a corporation could traffic in, a-personal and abstract (almost as though it were something which existed outside a mind, as though one could have knowledge without anybody to do the knowing – as Ramists were eventually to maintain one could). (1958: 152)

The Ramist spatialization and infinite binarization of the world, which Ong refers to as a 'corpuscular' episteme, haunts our educational apparatus to this day; the same technological drive toward efficiency that spawned textbooks on logic is now producing distance education and the ambitious electronic archiving projects that characterize much of humanities scholarship in the digital age.

As I argued in the previous chapter, the result of this 'fever for archiving' does not transform the humanities in any significant way or render humanities research more suitable to a culture of computing. New media have done little to alter the practices of humanities scholars, except perhaps by accelerating – by means of more accessible databases – the rate at which hermeneutics can be performed. Once again, I should stress the point that I am interested less in hermeneutics (interpretation) than I am in heuretics (invention). More specifically, this book asks the following question: Just as Ramus's scholarly method had a great influence in shaping a print apparatus that has persisted for five centuries, might it not be possible to invent scholarly methods to shape the digital apparatus?

Following Ulmer's approach to invention, my strategy is to draw on exemplars from our cultural history. Ulmer cites André Breton's co-option of Freud to invent surrealism. Since my goal is to invent a mode of discourse that challenges Ramist, print-based methods, I might very well co-opt a pre-Ramist methodology and ask the following question: Is it possible to do with Thomas Murner what André Breton did with Freud? Murner's reliance on iconography, for example, seems appropriate for the image-rich, iconic environment of computing. Furthermore, the non-sequential deck of cards is suggestive of the architecture of hypertext, an early instantiation of which is found in Apple's Hypercard software. Finally, Murner's integration of subjective mnemonic elements into the learning process is suggestive of computer interfaces, which lend themselves more to personalization and customization than to the hardened standardization of Ramist logic and print materiality.

While the materiality of Murner's *Logical Card Game* might serve as an adequate design exemplar for new media, Murner's scholarly method was not in itself revolutionary. In effect, Murner was doing precisely the same thing that many humanities scholars have dedicated their careers to today; he was transferring the practices of conventional scholarship (mnemonic topical logic) from one medium into a newer, more efficient medium. Ramus, by contrast, experimented simultaneously with method and materiality. As argued by Walter Ong,

> ... there is a regular progression [in Ramus's books] from early editions (wherein the text is a mass of typographical protoplasm, without running heads, without division into chapters or even into books, with little paragraphing, and almost no sense of spatial display) through later editions (where centered headings, running heads, and the other techniques of typographical display become more and more evident), to the *ne plus ultra* in commitment to space found in the editions in dichotomized outline form. (1958: 311)

Hence, as Ulmer has argued, we are now waiting for the Ramus (or Rami) of the late print culture to invent a new apparatus of pedagogy and scholarship, a new *ne plus ultra* in commitment to electronic space. The heuretic method suggests that we start by finding an appropriate exemplar, and so I turn, not to Murner or Ramus, but to a more visionary iconographer.

Books for Little Boys and Girls: William Blake

She is standing by the child with one hand on either side of his head (fig. 3.4). Is she lovingly preening the child's hair or sizing up his cranium? Is this a menacing image of harsh discipline or a comforting depiction of maternal benevolence? These are some of the questions provoked by William Blake's 'Nurse's Song,' from *Songs of Experience*, which, like Magritte's *La trahison des images*, can be seen as a hypericon, an image that 'encapsulates an entire episteme, a theory of knowledge' (Mitchell 1994: 49). Like Magritte's painting (a pipe accompanied by the words 'ceci n'est pas une pipe' or 'this is not a pipe'), the nurse hypericon encapsulates the integral ambivalence of image-texts, where words and images engage in an endless contest for meaning. For readers who see the nurse as a loving figure, a sampling of the accompanying poem proves shocking:

> Then come home, my children, the sun is gone down,
> And the dews of night arise;
> Your spring and your day are wasted in play,
>   And your winter and night in disguise.

Who could have imagined that such bitterness and cynicism would accom-

3.4 William Blake, 'Nurse's Song,' 1794: from *Songs of Innocence and of Experience*, copy Z, plate 38.

pany such a seemingly innocuous graphic? As in the case of Magritte's hypericon, we are led to ask the following: What are we supposed to believe, the image or the text? But I want to consider 'Nurse's Song' as an altogether different type of hypericon, one that not only encapsulates the infinite dissemination of meanings wrought by an imagetext, but that, conversely, also points to the delimiting restrictiveness of the print apparatus. This restrictiveness is most evident in the text, where the nurse's ultra-practicality seeks to wrench the children from their frivolous play and bind them into more serious, logical pursuits. But in order to invent this second hypericon, I have to dwell on the details of the image: the containment of the foregrounded child's head; the restraint of the same child's posture; the child in the background, enframed by a doorway, who appears to be reading. Not untypical of Romantic imagery, this is a scene of children coming into experience, being forced to abandon the (admittedly romanticized) innocence, creativity, and jubilation of childhood. The nurse and Peter Ramus shared the same pedagogic agenda.

While Blake is not considered a pedagogue in the same sense as Ramus or Murner, his penchant for producing children's books is indicative of a pedagogical sensibility – one that rejected ultra-logical forms of education. 'Nurse's Song' is merely one manifestation of Blake's incessant battle against educational practices (both informal, as practised by parents and nurses, and formal as in the Royal Academy) that privileged imitation over invention, and held reason above creativity. In Blake's philosophy, ultra-rational education was merely a symptom of a culture obsessed with Baconian reason:

> The child springs from the womb. the father stands ready to form
> The infant head while the mother idle plays with her dog on her couch
> The young bosom is cold for lack of mothers nourishment & milk
> Is cut off from the weeping mouth with difficulty & pain
> The little lids are lifted & the little nostrils opend
> The father forms a whip to rouze the sluggish senses to act
> And scourges off all youthful fancies from the newborn man
> Then walks the weak infant in sorrow compelld to number footsteps
> Upon the sand. &c (*Tiriel*, in Blake 1988: 285)

While this violent image of the 'formation' of an infant's head seems purely metaphorical, there is potential for a literal reading here. In *Émile*, Rousseau berates the practice of giving 'the heads of infants a more proper form by a sort of moulding,' a procedure that sometimes accompanied swaddling and tight-laced stays (1762–3: 11). Still, it was the mental swaddling of the infant – the practice of forcing children to 'number footsteps upon the sand' rather than allowing them to wander freely on the seashore –

that was the true crime in the eyes of Blake and Rousseau. The Romantic attitude toward the education of children is best exemplified in Rousseau's conception of the 'order of Nature':

> If, instead of transporting the mind of your pupil to a distance; if, instead of incessantly leading him astray in other places, in other climates, in other centuries, to the extremities of the earth, and even into the heavens, you make it your study to make him always self-contained and attentive to whatever immediately affects him – then you will always find him capable of perception, of memory, and even of reasoning: this is the order of Nature. (1762–3: 83–4)

The word 'self-containment' is instructive here. Permitting a child to be 'self-contained' is the very opposite of containing a child within the educational restraints of some sort of empirical apparatus.

The contemporary religious connotation of 'footsteps in the sand,' as quoted from *Tiriel* above, is a reminder that in the time of Blake and Rousseau empirical methods of childhood education ran alongside, and often went hand in hand with, a neo-Calvinist ideology. According to the Puritans of Blake's time, children were brought into the world in a state of Original Sin, and only a strict moral education could put them on the right path. Some empiricists, such as John Locke, sided with Rousseau and attempted to dispel the notion that children were innately evil and required containment. Yet the Lockean conception of the child's mind as a 'white Paper or Wax to be moulded' advocates educational restraint and containment as well. In response to the harsh, religious constraints of Puritan worshippers, Locke and his colleagues could offer only a sort of reason worship: an infant, according to Locke, 'as soon as he is capable of submission,' should learn to 'stand in Awe' of the father, 'in whose Power he is,' and by this means, be moulded into an 'obedient subject' (Leader 1981: 13). Hence, when Mrs Barbauld advises parents to 'impress devotional feelings as early as possible on the infant mind' (1781: v–vi), she is performing an agreeable marriage of Puritan and Lockean concepts of childhood education. One view organized the world into Good and Evil, the other into True and False; both advocated a strict containment of the child by instructing him/her to scorn the latter halves of these two oppositions.[3] Evidently, Blake could not subscribe to either of these philosophies, and he strove to eradicate both of them through his composite art.

Blake's most renowned work of composite art that might be viewed as an educational children's book is *The Songs of Innocence*, first published by his own relief-etch method in 1789. There are myriad possible reasons why Blake might have chosen to write a children's book, some more plausible than others. Perhaps the most tenable reason has to do with Blake's profession as an engraver and the artistic circle, hosted by his benefactors, Mr and Mrs A.S. Mathew, which he frequented as a young student. In the drawing room of Mrs Mathew, Zachary Leader notes, Blake may likely have met, among others,

Mrs Barbauld, who by 1781 had already published the popular *Lessons for Children from Two to Three Years Old* (1780) and *Hymns in Prose for Children* (1781); Mrs Chapone, part-author of number 10 of *The Rambler*, poetess, and published 'improver of young minds'; Mrs Montague, witty and articulate defender of Shakespeare against Voltaire, and patroness of chimney sweepers or 'climbing boys'; and Hannah More, friend, like Mrs Montague and Chapone, of Johnson and Garrick, tragic playwright, and author and founder of the immensely influential 'Cheap Repository Tracts' (1795–8), a scheme to provide suitable reading matter for the poor and their children. (1981: 2)

Besides keeping Blake well informed of the children's literary scene, these social connections led to commissions for the young engraver, among them, one from Samuel Johnson in 1780 to engrave Thomas Stothard's designs for *The Speaker: or Miscellaneous Pieces Selected from the Best English Writers, and disposed under proper heads, with a view to facilitate the Improvement of Youth in Reading and Speaking*. As we might expect from the conspicuously Ramist (n.b.: 'proper heads') title of this book, Mrs Mathew's circle, and the commissions that it generated for Blake, would prove to be a source of inspiration for him. But certainly they would not be a resource for emulation.

In 1784, Blake completed his first extended literary work, a burlesque drama that he called *An Island in the Moon*. While this nonsensical tale aims more at satirizing the bookshop of Joseph Johnson than it does 'Mrs Mathew's drawing room,' it is a clear indication of Blake's increasing disdain for mechanization, rigid orthodoxy, and reason worship, especially as applied to the instruction of children.[4] The satiric bite of this burlesque text confronts the reader quite brusquely at the very beginning of the tale:

In the Moon is a certain Island ... which ... seems to have some affinity to England, & what is even more extraordinary the people are so much alike & their language so much the same that you would think you was among your friends. (Blake 1988: 449)

Although such a 'booby-trap' beginning, as Geoffrey Summerfield calls it, would cause bells to go off in the head of the least satirically minded reader, this may not be the case if the reader is a child. *An Island in the Moon*, like many other satirical texts, from *Gulliver's Travels* to *Animal Farm*, works on a variety of levels, at least some of which can be appreciated by children. This concern for couching political and cultural critique in a form suitable for both children and adults is yet one more reason why Blake may have chosen to write children's books.

For Blake, it was not sufficient that a work should be appreciated by two distinct audiences, at least not in the sense that *Bugs Bunny* or *The Simpsons*, for example, can be appreciated by children exclusively for their slapstick chicaneries, and by adults for their intertextual, often political, allusions.

Although Blake was pleased by the fact that children had 'taken a greater delight in contemplating my Pictures than I ever hoped' (Blake 1988: 703), he wanted his art to cross the boundaries of perception. He wanted his adult readers to see like children, who, he said, 'can Elucidate my Visions' better than anyone (1988: 703). Why should Blake consider children as the critics who could best understand his 'Visions'? For an answer to this question, I turn to *The Marriage of Heaven and Hell*. If it is only through an 'increase in sensual enjoyment' that the world can appear 'infinite and holy' rather than 'finite and corrupt,' then children, indeed, are the human beings most likely to peer through the 'doors of perception' (Blake 1988: 39). To them, the world is an infinite source of sensual delight. Children, in the words of Zachary Leader, 'people their world with imaginary friends and foes, half-create what they see, animate inanimate objects, and take a spontaneous and unselfconscious delight in creation' (1981: 29). Adults, on the other hand, are bound to conceptions of time and space, and subscribe to such notions as *practicality* and especially *sanity*. In Jerusalem, Blake tells us that

> He who would see the Divinity must see him in his Children
> One first, in friendship and love; then a Divine Family, and in the midst
> Jesus will appear; so he who wishes to see a Vision; a perfect Whole
> Must see it in its Minute Particulars. (Blake 1988: 249)

The idea, then, is not to force children into a state of adulthood, but, in what is now recognized as a Romantic trope, to rely on them as ambassadors to a world of 'vision.' Vision, here, should not be confused with 'visuality,' for the latter is only one facet of the visionary's sensual perception of reality.

A child's experience of the world should be considered in the context of Blake's 'Fourfold Vision.'[5] In *Blake's Composite Art*, W.J.T. Mitchell describes the 'Fourfold Vision' as 'the world as sensed through *all* the gates of the body, not merely the eyes; and in rhetorical terms, it is a way of improving the sensual enjoyment of his spectators, designing visual illusions which continually demand and imply all the other senses in their structures' (74). Of greatest importance here is the fact that Blake opposes his visionary sensuality to what he called 'Single vision & Newtons sleep':

> Now I a fourfold vision see
> And a fourfold vision is given to me
> Tis fourfold in my supreme delight
> And three fold in soft Beulahs night
> And twofold Always. May God us keep
> From Single vision & Newtons sleep. (Blake 1988: 722)

It is not the place of the father, then, to 'form a whip' and 'rouze the sluggish senses' of the child. The father who would do so is not an active pedagogue; he is rapt in a state of reason worship and needs to be roused from his condition of 'Single vision & Newtons sleep.'[6] Blake hoped to accomplish this rousing by means of a composite art form that compels the viewer to react on several different levels. 'Blake's pictorial style,' Mitchell suggests,

> like his poetic form and the total form of his composite art, is organized as a dramatic, dialectical interaction between contrary elements. His poems present the drama of consciousnesses interacting with themselves, with others, and with a malleable, nonobjective environment. His pictures present the dramatic interaction of bodies with one another and with the immediate, multisensory elements of existential (not visual) space. (1978: 74)

In other words, Blake's works of composite art might not arouse our senses of smell, taste, and touch, but he invites us to engage with his prints on something other than a visual level; his work compels us to react in ways that might altogether change the way in which we *see* and experience the world. In Mitchell's terms, Blake's composite art, like his theory of 'contraries,' is a 'dialectic of dialectics,' a meeting of various opposing forces within a complex space of eternal conflict. This a long way from the Ramist notion of dialectic, the goal of which is to simplify all of the external world into hyper-organized, bracketed dichotomies, and to discipline the mind to be an a-personal container of information.

Digitization in the Age of Blake

Unlike other Romantics, such as Rousseau, Blake was not an outright anti-technologist; his critique targets the mechanistic techniques tied into the apparatus, and not the apparatus itself. Rather than rejecting the apparatus of print production, then, he chose to invent his own, based on techniques that subverted the dehumanizing potential of mechanical reproduction. The primary target of Blake's critique of education was the Royal Academy, led by Blake's whipping boy, Sir Joshua Reynolds. A sample of verse drawn from Blake's notebook indicates that he showed no restraint in berating the educational legacy of the Academy:

> You say their Pictures well Painted be
> And yet they are Blockheads you all agree
> Thank God I never was sent to school
>   To be Flogd into following the Style of a Fool (Blake 1988: 510)

Blake's railing against the 'blockheads' of his day achieved its highest pitch when he disparaged mechanistic engraving practices. In *The Counter-*

Arts Conspiracy: Art and Industry in the Age of Blake, Morris Eaves argues that 'the history of engraving recapitulates within print technology one version of the discovery of a workable digital principle that could be efficiently applied to the intractable problems of reproducing paintings' (186). 'Being digital,' then, does not necessarily have anything to do with being 'electronic' or being 'computer-centric.' As Eaves suggests, 'digitization is not a notion confined to electronic devices but a technological norm that operates across a spectrum of materials and processes. As a rule of thumb, the more deeply digitization penetrates, the more efficient the process becomes' (186). Ramus's corpuscular method, for example, is a superb example of how digital technology functions. Whereas Ramus spoke of 'dichotomies,' however, we might be more familiar with the term binaries. As in Ramist logic, in which information is reducible to the opposing branches of dichotomies, in the computer age all information is reducible to two bits, 1 and 0.

At the heart of digitization is a praxis of 'division' that Blake strived to denounce through his 'chaosthetics.' In the secular world, Blake associated this mechanization with Baconian or Newtonian science; in religion, he associated it with Puritanism; in the world of art and literature, he associated it, not with the printing press, but with mechanized methods of engraving. For Blake, the 'digital' engravings of Woollett, Strange, and Bartolozzi were the result of an ill-conceived, narrow-minded reductionism. As a radical alternative, he proposed his own 'infernal method' of relief-etch printing, which he used to create imagetexts that disrupted the tidiness of binary logic.

In *The Counter-Arts Conspiracy,* Eaves convincingly demonstrates Blake's disdain toward the 'undecided bungling' of 'journeymen' who possessed only a mechanical knowledge of the art of engraving. Dennis Read also helps clarify the concept of Blake as engraver in 'The Context of Blake's "Public Address": Cromek and the Chalcographic Society,' in which he outlines Blake's attempts to rescue the art of engraving (*chalcography*) from its conversion into a mechanical science. Indeed, the 'Public Address' (a montage of fragments from Blake's notebook, in which he defends – and even shamelessly advertises – his art, comparing and contrasting it to the work of several vogue Italians) reveals a great deal about Blake's campaign against mechanization and the thriving commercialism that it fostered. In the following passage, for example, it is commerce that is to blame for the mechanization of engraving and subsequent 'fatal' numbing of the English mind:[7]

> Englishmen rouze yourselves from the fatal slumber into which Booksellers & Trading Dealers have thrown you Under the artfully propagated pretence that a Translation or a Copy of any kind can be as honourable to a Nation as An Original. (Blake 1988: 576)

As several critics have pointed out – and this has become a primary focal point of Blake studies – Blake's method of relief etching was not as mechanized as such methods practised by Woollett, Strange, and others as mezzo-tint and stipple engraving. The difference lies mainly in the fact that Blake drew and painted the *graven* image directly on the plate before etching it, rather than using a technique in which the engraver broke the image into corpuscular units and transferred these onto a gridded plate by scratching out a series of lines and dots. Furthermore, each of Blake's prints had to be 'pulled' individually from the copper plate, and each print had to be touched up before being bound. This results, according to Stephen Leo Carr, in a 'radical variability' that characterizes Blake's art:

> For most works, both graphic and verbal, designed for mechanical reproduc-tion, variation from the primary text or master copy occurs as an undesirable intervention in the normal productive process, as an accidental departure from the original or an extra-ordinary revision by an author or editor of the initial invention. The logic of mechanical reproduction is one of identity: it leads to a multiplication of the same, to a mass publication of what are taken to be identi-cal copies. (1986: 182)

Although, as Joseph Viscomi has shown, Blake's printing method was sup-plemented by a necessary division of tasks (i.e., the etched plate had to be created first, the paper print second, and the painterly additions later), relief-etching is certainly a method that flies in the face of mechanization, and that necessarily allows for the inclusion of contingent elements, which would be unacceptable in a more efficient commercial process.

But it was not only the book dealers who were to blame for the increasing mechanization that Blake saw all around him. Although Blake does point the finger at commerce, he also notes that 'In a Commercial Nation Impost-ers are abroad in all Professions these are the greatest Enemies of Genius' (Blake 1988: 582). Among these impostors, of course, is that famous group of mechanizers, the Republic of Scholars. Although, as Dennis Read has pointed out, the Chalcographic Society was 'optimistically modelled in some respects on the plan of the British Institution' (1981: 75), we can be cer-tain that Blake would have had no part in an institution that mechanized knowledge acquisition. The British Institution, along with the Royal Acad-emy, were cogs in a machine that Morris Eaves has called the 'Counter-Arts,' the ideal form of which would be

> a macrosystem capable of unifying labor, management, marketers, and markets through interlocking structures that coordinate the ideological (such as a con-sensus about 'taste,' to supply ideas that legitimate material outcomes), the institutional (such as the Royal Academy and the British Institution, to supply formal education and display space), and the technological (such as the meth-ods and machines discussed below, to supply techniques of production) with the overarching socioeconomic framework. (1992: 176)

To call this ideal and all too familiar model of capitalism a 'conspiracy,' as Eaves does in the title of his book, is as tongue-in-cheeky as to call the late eighteenth century the 'Age of Blake'; but for Blake, this apparatus for mechanization must indeed have seemed conspiratorial, for its goal was to thwart all that he deemed as intelligent, artistic, and life-enhancing.

Blake's greatest contention with the Republic of Scholars as he knew it was its predilection for instructing students exclusively in the art of imitation.[8] Blake derided those who would take the designs of 'Rubens Rembrandt or Titian to turn that which is Soul & Life into a Mill or Machine.' For in Blake's mind, 'A Machine is not a Man nor a Work of Art it is Destructive of Humanity & of Art' (Blake 1988: 575). Although imitation is indeed part of an artist's early formation, the English School of Blake's time took it one step further, and automated painting and engraving into an assembly-line sort of process. In what Eaves has called the English School's 'sanctioned vertical eclecticism,' young artists were encouraged to combine 'the drawing of Raphael,' 'the coloring of Titian,' etc. into a finished product (1992: 259). Blake, however, viewed this penchant for 'eclecticism' as a 'commercial ploy to authorize an academic curriculum – to ensure an abundance of specialized expertise in the arts of imitation that are basic to all systematic pedagogy – that could in turn support a system of production organized to multiply copies through cheap divided labor' (237). The English School's attempt to keep up with the Latinate virtuosi through a synthesis of Continental techniques was, in Blake's mind, an education in ignorance, a mill for producing mental cripples, or 'blockheads': 'This is like what Sr. Francis Bacon says that a healthy Child should be taught & compelld to walk like a Cripple while the Cripple must be taught to walk like healthy people O rare wisdom' (Blake 1988: 580).

Much has been written about Blake's printmaking method, and to date the most extensive research into the subject has been undertaken by Joseph Viscomi, as outlined in his excellent study *Blake and the Idea of the Book*. Of greatest interest here, Viscomi identifies a twofold argument in Blake's apocalyptic imagetext, *Marriage of Heaven and Hell*. *Marriage* is simultaneously a critique of the Cartesian (and, I would add, Ramist) binarization of the world and a technical description of the materiality of Blake's mode of print production. The following passage – which has been filtered down to popular culture through Aldous Huxley and Jim Morrison – should provide an apt illustration of this layered fusion of form and content:

> The ancient tradition that the world will be consumed in fire at the end of six thousand years is true. as I have heard from Hell. For the cherub with his flaming sword is hereby commanded to leave his guard at the tree of life, and when he does, the whole creation will be consumed, and appear infinite, and holy whereas it now appears finite and corrupt.

This will come to pass by an improvement of sensual enjoyment. But first the notion that man has a body distinct from his soul, is to be expunged; this I shall do, by printing in the infernal method, by corrosives, which in Hell are salutary and medicinal, melting apparent surfaces away, and displaying the infinite which was hid.

If the doors of perception were cleansed every thing would appear to man as it is: infinite.

For man has closed himself up, till he sees all things thro' narrow chinks of his cavern. (Blake 1988: 39)

Blake's relief-etching method involved painting with acid-resistant ink on a copper plate, and then immersing that plate into a bed of acid, a process that would melt away surfaces to 'display the infinite' of Blake's imagetexts. As argued by Viscomi and other Blake scholars before him, Blake's reference to 'corrosives ... melting apparent surfaces away' underscores the degree to which the materiality of his mode of production was etched into his visionary philosophy.[9]

In Romantic studies this passage has not been perceived solely as a metaphor for Blake's mode of production; others have considered the manner in which it resonates with what some might call Blake's *episteme of the contraries*. Blake's suggestion that body and soul are not distinct entities tempts us, at once, to pigeonhole him as an anti-Cartesian or, more appropriately, as an anti-Platonist and an anti-Christian. But in essence, Blake does not discard any episteme entirely. Instead, he challenges specific tendencies of Christianity and Platonism, while maintaining concepts that are unquestionably Christian or Platonic. Most specifically, Blake expels the tendency of simplifying the world into binary oppositions for the sake of creating a homogeneous vision that chooses one moral path over another. Blake describes this homogenization as 'Negation,' and, as we learn over and over again, in *The Marriage of Heaven and Hell*, for example, he regards it as inhumane: 'One law for the Lion & Ox is Oppression' (Blake 1988: 44). Whereas Negation brings binary oppositions together so that one may cross out the other to achieve 'sameness,' Blake's concept of 'contraries' points to a difference that cannot, and never should be, resolved. And it is this irresolution, this clashing of differences, that Blake sees as the energy-source of all life. In a passage from *Milton*, the blind bard tells Ololon that

There is a Negation, & there is a Contrary
The Negation must be destroyd to redeem the
   Contraries
The Negation is the Spectre; the Reasoning Power
   in Man
This is a false Body ... (Blake 1988: 142)

Morris Eaves has suggested that 'negations,' in Blake's episteme, 'aim to destroy contrariety, the ongoing constructive *process* of mental opposition, and thus aim to replace useful difference with a dominance of the same' (1992: 149). Contraries, then, must be considered as an 'eternal operating principle' (149). Even 'the Reasoning Power in Man' – which is often considered as Blake's ideological nemesis and lyrical whipping boy – has a place in his radical dialectic, for 'Without Contraries is no progression. Attraction and Repulsion, Reason and Energy, Love and Hate, are necessary to Human existence. Good is the passive that obeys Reason. Evil is the active springing from Energy' (Blake 1988: 34).

This notion of contraries vs. negations can be confusing since it seems to suggest at once that Blake is a Nietzschean precursor, a sort of anarchist beyond good and evil, but that he also aspires toward an ideal aesthetic in which good and evil exist, but interact productively. W.J.T. Mitchell, for example, suggests that

> for Blake, the dualistic world of mind and body, time and space, is an illusion which must not be imitated, but is to be dispelled by the processes of his art ... Relief etching with acid or 'corrosives' was the process by which Blake cut his copper plates, melting away the apparent surface of the copper to reveal an art form in which soul and body, rendered in the modalities of poetic time and pictorial space, are united ... Blake sees the separation of body and soul, space and time, as various manifestations of the fall of man, 'His fall into Division' (*FZ* 4:4). (1978: 31)

Contraries may oppose one another, but they are not to be separated or divided into immutable categories or headings as in, for example, the Ramist dichotomization of knowledge. Nor are the contraries to be reconciled for the sake of sameness, but wedded in an eternally antagonistic marriage. The yin/yang icon comes to mind here. Blake may not be Nietzschean at all, then, for he chose to retain the categories of good and evil. However, he did so only in order to deconstruct the categories. What matters most for the sake of this study is not whether Blake is beyond such contraries as 'good and evil,' but to recognize that Blake's work, informed by his notion of the 'contraries,' involves a unification of form and content, material production and ideology.

An excellent example of how contraries function is in the imagetext, that enigmatic space in which word and picture meet, but never reconcile, for they are bound in a dialectical relationship in which 'neither can be reduced to the other's terms' (Magritte, in Foucault 1982: 9). It is the imagetext, of course, that best defines the products of Blake's relief-etching method, a bringing together of body and soul, word and picture, into a space where 'a virtual and supplementary sensuality emerges' (Kittler 1990: 6). Like the

3.5   William Blake, *The Angel Michael Binding Satan* ('He Cast him into the Bottomless Pit, and Shut him up'), c. 1800.

modernist artists examined by Johanna Drucker in *The Visible Word*, Blake 'pushes alphabetic writing toward the realm of pictorial values, asking us to see his alphabetic forms with our senses, not just read through or past them to the signified speech or "concept" behind them, but to pause at the sensuous surface of calligraphic and typographic forms' (Mitchell 1994: 147). What Blake and the modernists after him were calling for is a more concerted focus on, and control of, the shift between figure and ground in visual communication, a concept that I focus on in the next chapter.

As an example of how this 'dialectics of dialectics' functions through Blake's composite art, consider Blake's 'Nurse's Song' (fig. 3.4). In order to demonstrate Blake's dialectical art to students in a 'Survey of British Literature' course, I removed the text from the image and posted the 'de-texted' plate (an imagetext converted into an image) on the Web as part of an assignment entitled 'Re-writing Blake.' As the instructions to the exercise indicate, the students were asked to 'fill in the blank writing space on the plate by describing exactly' what they saw in the picture. This task included the following steps:

1. 'steal' the image from the page I have created;
2. use image editing software to inscribe your words directly in the blank space on the image;
3. publish the plate on the Web and send the URL to the class list for discussion.

The goal of the project was not for the students to be poetic, nor was it, at least in the first instance, to quiz them on their memorization of Blake's *Songs* or on the historical context of his work; in fact, I sprung this project on them a week before the students were supposed to begin studying the *Songs* – insurance that they were coming to the plates with a certain innocence regarding the subject. The goal was to investigate subject positioning, stereotyping, the interaction of word and image, and the nature of human perception.

Each group completed the assignment within an hour, and we then examined the results by comparing their work to the unaltered plates. In several cases, the students were astounded by the fact that Blake's poem delivered a very different message than the one they had written to match the picture. Most of the groups who *rewrote* 'Nurse's Song' described the picture as a peaceful domestic scene in which a mother or female caretaker is grooming a child, who they erroneously assumed was a female.[10] They put no effort into describing the minute particulars of the plate because they viewed the scene as cliché, something to be taken for granted. But when they first saw a copy of the complete facsimile, in which the nurse tells the children, 'Your spring and your day are wasted in play / And your winter and night in disguise,' it was as if the picture had undergone some sort of transformation. After observing the complete facsimile, with its dismal connotations, many stu-

3.6 William Blake, 'Nurse's Song,' 1794 (text removed).

dents commented on the details with a greater degree of care. For example, several students noted that the positioning of the Nurse's hands seemed awkward and unnatural. They suggested that the nurse appears to be 'measuring the child's head,' or at least 'containing it' within the makeshift frame of her hands. They also noticed that the child seems somewhat constrained, standing as he is with his arms crossed awkwardly about his torso. The whole scene, one group of students would suggest later, reminded them of Wordsworth's 'We Are Seven,' in which, as we had concluded in a previous class, a rational, *experienced* adult tries and fails to impose his conception of death on a pre-rational, *innocent* child.

Some students decided to continue this discussion on the class listserv. Here is an example of what one student wrote:

> I thought it was rather interesting how people could see one thing in the plates when they didn't know what they were about and then another when they were told what it actually was. It was like all of a sudden they had seen that all along. It was strange that when told what something is supposed to be, everyone almost automatically adapts their perception to see it that way. It's also kind of a good thing because it also shows that people are willing to keep an open mind and see things in another person's view.

Through this exercise, Blake teaches us a dialectical lesson in perspective. Mainly, he teaches us not to trust our visual sense alone – an invaluable lesson for students bombarded daily by the words and images of a postmodern mediascape in which the imagetext is the dominant mode of communication. Like Magritte's *Trahison des images*, Blake's 'Nurse's Song,' through a radical dialectic of image and text, causes us to reconsider our own subject positioning, to question the faculties and strategies by means of which we experience and organize the world.

Of course, 'Re-writing Blake' is only a simple exercise – one which some may rightly consider 'un-extraordinary' – created for first-year students in a survey class. But even though this exercise may not be revolutionary in itself, it is an indication that new media, when used for something other than archival purposes (in effect, this exercise in digital graffiti might not please the guardians of the Blake Archive), may serve as a means of rousing ourselves from the 'Single vision & Newtons sleep' in which print technology has steeped us. By creating exercises such as 'Re-writing Blake,' instructors are not asking students to write *about* the poet/painter; they are asking students to write *with* him. Students are asked to engage in a method of composition that deviates from the discourse of the Republic of Scholars. This poetics of 'writing with,' practised in a new media environment, is a way of inventing new discursive practices suitable to an age of computing. In the final chapter, I will consider the possibility of carrying this poetics, a poetics of the hypericon, into the space of the Web. There, it will be reconsidered according to a dialectic of figure/ground, author/reader, and self/other, always reaching toward a mode of representation that cautiously embraces the capacaties of new technology, while loosening the cognitive vise of the printing press and its consequent, conspiratorial methodologies.

New Media for Everyone: Hypericonomy

As I noted earlier, Lev Manovich has made the suggestion that the inventors of a language of new media might follow a 'writing with' strategy, a suggestion which is worthy of quoting again here:

> ... by looking at the history of visual culture and media, in particular, cinema, we can find many strategies and techniques relevant to new media design. Put differently, to develop a new aesthetics of new media, we should pay as much attention to cultural history as to the computer's unique new possibilities to generate, organize, manipulate, and distribute data. (2000: 314)

I would argue that humanities scholars should not limit themselves to modernism and the cinema in the search for 'media exemplars.' For my own purposes, the radical matrix in Blake's work of form and content, of philosophy and materiality, along with his turn against the dehumanizing potential of new technologies and, most importantly, against a techno-bureaucratic version of education, provide an ideal exemplar for inventing a new method and materiality suitable to the current apparatus of computing. The problem lies in designing such a 'technoromantic'[11] method.

In the opening chapter of this book, I promised to introduce a new, monstrous mode of academic discourse that I have dubbed 'hypericonomy.' In the simplest terms, hypericonomy might be defined as an economy of hypericons. My strategy has been to 'show' this method in this chapter rather than explain it away with a series of easily replicable instructions. In this way, I am attempting to provoke a certain degree of misunderstanding, with the hope that readers might produce their own monstrous versions of hypericonomy. This is a strategy that, in Ulmer's terms, is designed to trigger a *relay*. Still, I will offer readers a stereotypical 'origin story' of the method I propose here, in order to remind them that a hypericonomy should be generated subjectively, motivated by extreme affect, as are medieval or early modern mnemonic devices (after all, most inventions have convenient origin stories – Newton and the apple, Archimedes in the bathtub, etc.).

Throughout this essay, I have moved across levels of discourse, following the 'vise.' The notion of constructing an economy of hypericons as a research methodology came to me in an 'aha' moment after watching the film *Casino*. I was particularly struck by the scene in which Nicky Santoro, played by Joe Pesci, turns Tony Doggs into an information database by putting his head in a vise:

NICKY SANTORO: Listen to me Anthony. I got your head in a fuckin' vise. I'll
squash your head like a fuckin' grapefruit if you don't give me a name.

It was not just the gratuitous violence of the scene that struck me, but the fact
that I was reminded of the time my own brother threatened to put my head
in a vise, inspired by the Three Stooges' antics, which we often watched
together on television after coming home from grade school. Beginning with
this primal scene, I was able to piece together a *mystory* – a genre of writing
that I will outline in greater detail in the final chapter – drawing on the discourses of personal history, collective history, academic discipline, and popular culture. The mystorical *popcycle* that I developed in this particular case
looked something look this:

Personal: my brother's attempt to put my head in a vise.
History: the invention of the printing press.
Discipline: the art of William Blake, particularly 'Nurse's Song.'
Pop Culture: the Three Stooges, or *Casino* scene of a head in a vise.

The image of a head in a vise provided me with a visual puncept to link
together the various elements of this mystory (and also provided me with a
way of organizing this chapter). It is this notion of a 'visual puncept' that is
at the root of hypericonomy, and which is also akin to the aesthetic techniques of William Blake. I have converted this mystory into essay form in
this chapter. The essay is performing itself through this imagery.
   In *William Blake's Composite Art*, W.J.T. Mitchell proposes the idea that
Blake's imagery can be understood in terms of a fourfold schema of shapes
that the artist drew upon to rouse the senses of the viewer: circle/orb/eye;
spiral/vortex/ear; arabesque/*S*-curve/tongue; arch/inverted *U*/nose (65).
According to Mitchell, Blake's use of the schemata enables him to induce a
visionary effect on the viewer – it is a way of arguing and provoking by
means of repeated image patterns:

> If pictures are like sensory openings or perceptual structures, then looking at
> them is like putting on a new pair of spectacles or (more precisely) like opening
> your eyes. In other words, Blake's style, like that of any great artist, affects our
> vision: we start seeing vortices and arches and wave forms everywhere, in and
> out of Blake's pictures. (68)

Hypericonomy borrows from Blake this strategy of pattern recognition for
the purpose of building an argument that will impact the vision of the reader.
Of course, hypericonomy also borrows from the pictorial logic of advertising
and of Hollywood film, both of which assail us with the repetition of icons on
a daily basis. The feedback loop between the Three Stooges scene, the incident
with my brother, and the *Casino* scene is indicative of the process of subject

formation in a culture saturated with endlessly repeated broadcast images. Those who engage in hypericonomy are asked to take a more critical look at that mode of subject formation, and have the opportunity to short-circuit it by producing and broadcasting their own schematic sets of icons – not for the sake of marketing and sales, however, but for the sake of education.

To quote loosely the various corporate icons, academic visionaries, and software commercials that are part of my own subjectivity: in a rapidly trans-forming digital culture, specialization is a liability (just ask any student who has recently graduated from computer science or engineering); multitasking, dabbling, and autodidaction are the order of the day. Most computer users are not artists, for example, but they engage in artistic practices. They approach graphic design from the position of amateurs or dilettantes, cobbling together design elements by using the electronic tools that are at their disposal. To put this essay together, I scanned images from books, 'stole' images off the Web, cropped and resized them in Photoshop, and finally imported them into my Microsoft Word document. By engaging in this activity of bricolage, I am entering into the economy of image production, which is traditionally rele-gated to artists and heavily protected by copyright laws. I certainly may not have the specialized skills to create an icon, but I do have the necessary tools to create a hypericon or even an economy of hypericons, although this requires me to break print-oriented laws of ownership and distribution. It is in this focus on dilettantism that hypericonomy reflects the holistic method-ology of William Blake; that is, the material production process of hypericon-omy complements its philosophy, which is one of decompartmentalization.

Digital media aficionados might protest that the version of hypericonomy that I have offered in this chapter is not suitable to a 'digital age' or is not 'cyber' enough because it was destined for print production. I would remind these critics that *remediation*, a term coined by Jay Bolter and Richard Grusin to designate the co-opting of one media form by another (e.g., the Web-like appearance of CNN), can go both ways. As Espen Arseth demonstrates in *Cybertext: Perspectives on Ergodic Literature*, print works such as the *I Ching* and Raymond Queneau's *Cent Mille Milliards* qualify as cybertexts. Furthermore, Katherine Hayles argues in *Writing Machines* that a technotext, a work that 'interrogates the inscription technology that produces it,' does not have to find its materiality in electronic media. The work of William Blake, the media exemplar I have chosen in the invention of hypericonomy, is a case in point. Hayles points to such technotexts as Mark Z. Daneilewski's *House of Leaves* and Johanna Drucker's *Otherspace: Martian Ty/opography.* Still, since one goal of this book is to provoke the invention of new scholarly methods suitable to an age of computing, in the following chapters I will offer samples of what hypericonomy might look like as a digital media practice. But that will require a hypericonic shift from the vise to the magnifying glass, and more generally, a continual and deliberate shifting between figure and ground in scholarly discourse.

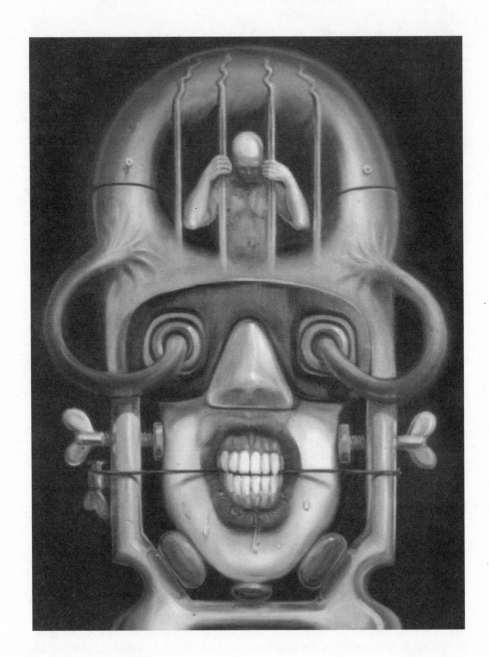

3.7 Stephen Gibb, *No Parole*, 1990.

4. NONSENSE AND PLAY:
The Figure/Ground Shift in New Media Discourse

The end of linear writing is indeed the end of the book, even if, even today, it is within the form of a book that new writings – literary or theoretical – allow themselves to be, for better or for worse, encased. It is less a question of confiding new writings to the envelope of a book than of finally reading what wrote itself between the lines in the volumes. That is why, beginning to write without the line, one begins also to reread past writing according to a different organization of space. If today the problem of reading occupies the forefront of science, it is because of this suspense between two ages of writing. Because we are beginning to write, to write differently, we must reread differently.

– Jacques Derrida, *Of Grammatology,* 86–7

Visualization and Intelligence

A few years ago, while chaperoning a group of Grade 8 students on a field trip, I had the opportunity to visit the Sega Playdium in Mississauga, Ontario. The Playdium is an imposing forty-thousand-square-foot structure containing over two-hundred video games and simulators.[1] Admittedly, I was impressed by the sheer magnitude and electronic sophistication of this warehouse of digital simulacra. As a child, I had felt the rush of electronic, immersive entertainment, which at the time meant TV and an Atari 2600 video game system. But the immersive environments of Playdium are galaxies away from those skittish, two-dimensional 2600 games such as *Pitfall* and *Pole Position*. Perhaps this is why, upon entering the Playdium, I chose to bypass the high-tech games like *Solar Assault* and *Mortal Kombat 4* (games that will be clearly outdated by the time this book is printed), and went straight to a traditional marksman's game called *Police Trainer*. I could tell that this game – hidden away in the furthest corner of the Playdium, unattended by the usual anxious queue of jittery adolescents – was a real dud.

Not intimidated by the uncoolness of this game, I inserted my complimentary 'unlimited play' pass and began shooting.

Police Trainer is conceptually simple. The screen displays a variety of shooting galleries, and the player takes aim at the targets using a frighteningly realistic handgun attached to the machine by a cable. The galleries are organized into such categories as 'Speed' (targets appear at random on the screen, then disappear quickly), 'Marksmanship' (a variety of human silhouettes appear on the screen – 'bad guys' must be shot, 'good guys' spared), and 'Intelligence' (the screen is split horizontally with several targets on top and only one on the bottom – the player must shoot the target in the upper section that matches the single target in the lower section). 'Intelligence?' I asked myself. 'What does this have to do with intelligence?' I asked this, not because I was affronted by my incapacity to shoot accurately in this gallery (in fact, I did surprisingly well for an 'old man' – I was twenty-seven at the time), but because there seemed to be no possible correlation between a person's IQ and his/her ability to shoot a target on a video terminal. All this game requires, it seemed, is hand-eye coordination and the ability to visually zoom in on a limited field of pixels. Only a few days later, as I browsed through a copy of *American Scientist*, the correlation between *Target Practice* and 'intelligence' became as clear as the sky in the background of *Solar Assault*.

Only recently have we begun to see quantifiable evidence of the influence of electronic media on students in higher education. The Nintendo Generation, after all, has just begun to graduate, and rumours about TV-junkie or Net-addicted students with poor writing skills and short attention spans have not yet been treated with the attention of a widespread and unyielding crisis. We are quick to blame the shortfalls of the postmodern student on our visual culture, on television and video games, even on advertisements, comic books, and billboards. In the foreboding words of Neil Postman (which one could easily update to include computers), 'the decline of a print-based epistemology and the accompanying rise of a television-based epistemology has had grave consequences for public life ... We are getting sillier by the minute' (1986: 24). Even W.J.T. Mitchell, in his optimistic diagnosis of the 'pictorial turn,' concedes that 'everyone knows that television is bad for you and that its badness has something to do with the passivity and fixation of the spectator' (1994: 2). But what if television, playing video games, and surfing the Web are actually good for you? What if exercising the modes of cognition demanded by visually sophisticated video game and Web environments could actually increase one's intelligence?

In the aforementioned issue of *American Scientist*, Ulric Neisser makes this very argument as he raises the widely discussed issue of the 'Flynn effect,' a title given to identify the steady increase in IQ scores since the first tests were administered. Neisser argues, though guardedly, that visual media may be a substantial contributing factor in this pervasive increase. According to the Flynn effect (named after James Flynn, a political scientist at the University of Otago in New Zealand), we are not getting sillier at all. In fact, 'the rate of gain on standard broad-spectrum IQ tests amounts to three IQ points per decade, and it is even higher on certain specialized measures' (Neisser 2003). To explain this phenomenon, Neisser considers a broad range of factors, the most convincing of which is that 'children attend school longer now and have become more familiar with the testing of school-related material.' This explanation is unsatisfactory, however, since the increase in IQ scores is due mainly to improvements in non-academic areas, such as abstract and visual reasoning. In fact, Neisser points out that 'the tests more closely linked to school content show the smallest gains of all.' This leads him to conclude that the rise in IQ scores must be attributable to extra-scholarly phenomena, and after exploring the effects of 'nutrition' and 'child-rearing practices' on IQ scores, Neisser concludes that perhaps the most striking twentieth-century change in our cognitive environment, and hence the most viable explanation for the Flynn effect, is an increase in exposure to many types of visual media. 'From pictures on the wall to movies to television to video games to computers, each successive generation has been exposed to far richer optical displays than the one before.' Could our visual culture, then, the culture which is making us 'sillier by the minute,' actually be responsible for a certain intellectual (r)evolution? The pedagogical avant-garde, from the U.S. Army to the Baby Einstein Company, seem to think so.

Citing the work of Patricia Greenfield at UCLA, Neisser argues that children exposed to rich optical displays 'develop specific skills of visual analysis, skills in which they routinely excel their elders.' These skills go beyond the ability to program a DVD player or work a mouse, and although we might immediately think of the lessons of *Sesame Street* and *The Magic School Bus* (they assail our children on all sides – in books, on television, CD-Rom, and the Web) as the factors most likely to pump up an infant's brain, the cognitive skills which Greenfield identifies fall more generally into the category of 'visual analysis.' Visual analysis is a mode of cognition which is not generally developed by means of educational 'lessons' such as those provided in the content of these popular children's shows. Hence, these programs play only a marginal role in the Flynn effect, or, more accurately, it is not the traditional educational elements of these programs which account for the increased IQs, but the playful and visually rich environment in which these elements are communicated.

In a pictorial culture, as I have already suggested, 'visual analysis' is perhaps the most active mode of cognition, and it is called into action incessantly. But this optical mode goes beyond a passive fascination with the image as described, for example, by Neil Postman. 'Beyond merely looking at pictures,' Neisser observes that

we analyze them. Picture puzzles, mazes, exploded views and complex montages appear everywhere – on cereal boxes, on McDonald's wrappers, in the

4.1 Wendy and Michael Magnifier, 1998: McDonald's *Peter Pan* Happy Meal toy.

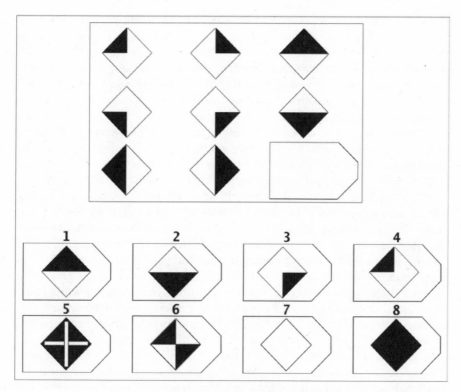

4.2 Raven test problem illustrating the 'figure addition rule.' In each row, the figures
from columns 1 and 2 are superimposed to obtain the figure from column 3. The
correct answer for the third row is 8.[2]

instructions for assembling toys and in books intended to help children pass the
time ... And static displays such as pictures are only the beginning. We have had
movies since the 1920s, television since the 1950s and video games since the
1970s. (Neisser 2003)

Neisser concludes that this postmodern penchant for play-like 'visual analysis' performs a determinant role in the Flynn effect, especially when we consider the increased scores on tests such as 'Raven's Progressive Matrices,'
which consists mainly of the spatial manipulation of geometrical shapes,
and which is used to measure abstract-reasoning ability.

By considering the possibility of a correlation between the Flynn effect and
developments in visual media, we are at least 'focusing our attention on the
diversity of mental abilities' and on the possibility that 'different forms of
intelligence are developed by different kinds of experience' (Neisser 2003).

Given this diversity, scholars and educators in all fields should consider it their responsibility to explore teaching practices that draw on and draw out modes of cognition other than the scholarly mode of storage/recall by means of which the academy measures intelligence. My argument, then, is not that visual media have made us, or our children, more intelligent than our predecessors, but that developments in the materiality of media lead to shifts in the hierarchy or matrix of cognitive processes.[3] And so, while we may be lax 'with respect to other aspects of intelligence,' we are 'indeed very much smarter than our grandparents where visual analysis is concerned' (Neisser 2003). Rather than hiding our electronic enlightenment under a bushel, then, perhaps we should be plying our advanced visual skills in the classroom.[4]

W.J.T. Mitchell suggests that 'people have always known, at least since Moses denounced the Golden Calf, that images were dangerous, that they can captivate the onlooker and steal the soul' (1994: 2). But if we learn to see this common knowledge as a cultural prejudice embedded within us by a five-hundred-year-old tradition of printed texts and the rule of reason, then we may begin to view the image as a tool for knowledge-acquisition, and not as a device for deception and depravity. If educators can get beyond this prejudice, then they can consider the possibility of drawing on other modes of cognition – more specifically 'visual analysis' – in scholarly circles, making use of the technology at our disposal. And they should do so, not out of a blind fascination and reverence for electronic tools, that is, because 'we have the technology' or because 'the media prescribe it' or, even worse, because 'it's fashionable'; we should draw more readily on these tools because they may provide us with a means of tapping into modes of cognition which evade the grasp of the Republic of Scholars – modes of cognition which break down the compartmentalization of knowledge, increase communication between student and instructor, and allow researchers to come to a better understanding of their subject matter, their culture, and themselves.

Achieving a shift between modes of cognition for pedagogical purposes is not a simple task, to say the least. Since I am not a cognitive psychologist, I will pursue this issue further, not by means of scientific research, but in terms more appropriate to humanities research; I will contextualize it within the fine arts concept of the shift between figure and ground. Rather than providing a precise recipe for achieving this shift, the following sections of this chapter provide exemplars that educators can draw upon in the development of their own educational practices.

Figure/Ground 1: The Optical Unconscious

In the first chapter, I looked at Rosalind Krauss's *The Optical Unconscious*, a remarkable study of modernity and the avant-garde. This text is of special interest to this study, not only because it sheds light on the avant-garde's attempts to form an 'alternative scopic regime,' but because Krauss emulates some of the very methods of avant-garde artists in an iconic, abyssal presentation of her research materials. Central to Krauss's methodology is a theory of 'visual analysis' with which the reader should now be familiar, a theory which depicts seeing as a subjective, intertextual activity. In the definition of *her own* 'optical unconscious,' Krauss speaks at once about this subjectivity and this intertextuality by means of which she sees the world of art and is able to write about it:

> If it [the optical unconscious] can be spoken of at all as externalized within the visual field, this is because a group of disparate artists have so constructed it there, constructing it as a projection of the way that human vision can be thought to be less than a master of all it surveys, in conflict as it is with what is internal to the organism that houses it. (1994: 179)

This 'group of disparate artists' to which Krauss refers is, of course, the twentieth-century avant-garde, whose compulsion to undo the visual prejudices of conventional modernism drove them to explore madness and childhood delirium.[5] Before examining the methods of the avant-garde, however, I would like to revisit the visual prejudices against which they were reacting. The *camera obscura*, as described by Krauss, might serve as a convenient hypericon[6] for encapsulating the classical understanding of visuality which the avant-garde challenged:

> Beaming light through a pinhole into a darkened room and focusing that light on the wall opposite, the camera obscura allowed the observer – whether it was Newton for his *Optics* or Descartes for his *Dioptique* – to view that plane as something independent of his own powers of synthesis, something that he, as a detached subject, could therefore observe. It was due to this structural disconnection between plane of focus and observing subject that the camera obscura came to function as a model for the 'classical' subject of knowledge. (1994: 128)

This classical model of visuality upholds the same approach to knowledge established by Ramus and his legacy of scholars, the same episteme which Blake scorned, and which he diagnosed as 'Single Vision and Newtons Sleep,' the same episteme that I will attempt to deconstruct here by means of a complexification.

Marcel Duchamp critiqued the 'single vision' of classical optics by identifying its guiding presence in certain types of modernist painting (i.e., impressionism, abstraction, cubism) and labelling it as 'retinalism,' a shallow attempt to appeal to the field of vision alone. 'Since the advent of impressionism,' Duchamp insisted, 'visual productions stop at the retina. Impressionism, fauvism, cubism, abstraction, it's always a matter of retinal painting.

Their physical preoccupations: the reactions of colors, etc., put the reactions of the gray matter in the background' (Krauss 1994: 128). Duchamp's response to this retinalism was to bring the 'reactions of the gray matter' to the foreground – a reconfiguring of artistic praxis, a shifting of figure and ground, form and content. Duchamp's yearning to foreground the 'gray matter' led ultimately to his experimentation with optical illusions (his *retrore-liefs*), which brought into relief the instability of the viewer's perspective, and, finally, the *Large Glass*, which he hoped would pierce through the retinal and reach viewers on a cognitive/psychic level. The *Large Glass*, according to Duchamp, required the viewer to experience the piece, not as a detached subject, but with all the 'density and opacity of the viewing subject as the very precondition of his access to sight' (Krauss 1994: 126).

Compared to the complexity of Duchamp's optical physics, the desire of the surrealists to foreground the unconscious may seem like elementary child's play. But it was indeed the surrealists and their 'child's play' which Duchamp most admired and wished to emulate, particularly their ability to toy with the figure/ground distinction. In *The Optical Unconscious*, Krauss relies heavily on the work of Max Ernst in order to demonstrate the surrealists' undoing of the figure/ground binary. In the following scene, Theodore Adorno takes the stage as a student of Ernst:

> Adorno is looking at the first plate of *Femme 100 têtes*, or perhaps, since they are identical, the last. 'Crime or miracle,' the initial caption reads, 'a complete man.' In its second, final, appearance the image is titled simply 'End and continuation.' But in each of the two identical plates, Blake's angel Gabriel, minus his trumpet, collaged against a stormy sky, is falling from the center of the large, egglike form of something that could be an ascending balloon. Or is he, too, like the souls he is calling forth on the last judgement, rising? The tiny men huddled below, in the windswept space of the nineteenth-century wood engraving, resemble indeed the populations of awakened dead from medieval tympana. At least in the grip of Adorno's associations, they do. (1994: 34)

In Ernst's collage – indeed, in a variety of plates from *La femme 100 têtes* – figure and ground shift and shimmer as they might in an optical illusion, undoing the stability of the viewer's perspective. From one point of view, Blake's angel Gabriel is the figure of the painting; from another, he 'is more like background, the single, grand surface on which everything else is supported. A foreground, then, that is also a background, a top that is clearly a bottom' (1994: 36). Through a variety of methods, surrealists attempted to undo basic assumptions about figure and ground, self and other, dreaming and 'reality,'[7] etc., all in the name of altering human perception. Whether or not they succeeded is in the eye of the beholder.

The fact that surrealism has made its way onto T-shirts, bumper stickers,

4.3 Max Ernst, 'Crime or Miracle: A Complete Man,' 1929.

advertisements, and even into contemporary humour[8] might be viewed as evidence that the surrealists' attempt to infiltrate social consciousness has been a success. A more acceptable view, however, is that surrealism has been commodified, tapped and drained of its shock effect, de- or perhaps *re*-politicized by a postmodern, capitalist market. In either case, the contemporary popularity of surrealist imagery, imagery which stunned and baffled its initial audience, demonstrates the advanced level of optical sophistication possessed by the average contemporary consumer.

Figure/Ground 2: Children's Literature

Not surprisingly, the surrealists looked to childhood experience as a means of transforming humanity's relationship to the everyday. In a preceding chapter, I suggested that a child's world is quite unlike that of an adult: children 'people their world with imaginary friends and foes, half-create what they see, animate inanimate objects, and take a spontaneous and unselfconscious delight in creation' (Leader 1981: 29). In their attempt to enter into this idealized childhood world, the surrealists took to game-playing, nonsensical babbling, intentional disorientation, etc.[9] In general, surrealism involved a sort of psychoanalytic revision of childhood experiences, not as a means of therapy, however, but in order to apply these experiences to the transformation of everyday life. Quoting Adorno once again, Krauss notes that surrealist technique is an attempt to 'uncover childhood experiences by blasting them out. What surrealism adds to the pictorial rendering of the world of things is what we lost after childhood' (1994: 34). Adorno then draws a comparison between the nonsensical illustrations in children's literature and the arcane pictorial inventions of the surrealists: '... when we were children those illustrations, already archaic, must have jumped out at us, just as the surrealistic pictures do now. The giant egg out of which the monster of the last judgement can be hatched at any minute is so big because we were so small when we for the first time shuddered before the egg' (34).

The affinity between surrealist art and children's literature has not gone unnoticed. In *Nonsense: Aspects of Intertextuality in Folklore and Literature*, for example, Susan Stewart takes a detailed look at both and notes their shared willingness to shatter figure/ground distinctions. Another way of looking at this undoing of figure and ground is to consider it as a changing of roles between frame and content. This shift can be achieved by considering the frame itself as content, an effect most commonly achieved by creating a 'frame within a frame' or a *mise en abyme* relationship between elements in an image or text. 'The frame-within-a-frame,' Krauss suggests,

> is a way of entering the figure into the pictorial field and simultaneously negating it, since it is inside the space only as an image of its outside, its limits, its frame. The figure loses its logical status as that object in a continuous field

which perception happens to pick out and thereby to frame; and the frame is no longer conceived as something like the boundary of the natural or empirical limits of the perceptual field. (1994: 16)

Put simply, one can reverse the conventional figure/ground relationship by putting greater emphasis on the frame,[10] or even on the act of enframing, rather than on the content of an image or text. Besides surrealist painting, this shift may be witnessed in 'the carnivalizing aspects of ritual, the novel that takes on all of language and the history of literature as its subject, [and in] many forms of children's speech play' (Krauss 1994: 21). Literature that mimics the nonsensical speech play of children might be considered as 'a text slipping through its frame, reinventing its limits in the same way that a trickster changes his shape' (91). Surrealist art, children's literature, and the playful activities of children themselves all perform a sort of Houdini-like trick by means of which figure and ground shift unpredictably, radically undermining our everyday, commonsensical understanding of reality.

All of these forms of nonsense are essential to this study since they provide examples of how to break out of the ultra-commonsensical circle of the Republic of Scholars. 'At the point of nonsense,' Stewart suggests, 'common sense is scattered and dispersed, made relative to alternative systems of order' (1978: 21). The univocal, authoritative discourse of the Republic of Scholars is threatened, of course, by the multivocal play of nonsense and its dispersive effect. Various instances of nonsense, such as the pun or the macaronic, can short-circuit the rational world and act as short cuts between worlds of experience. Put differently, nonsense creates 'a tear in the fabric of any singular way of organizing the world, in any ethnocentrism ... It is an encounter with the possibility of the "Unimaginable object" through an alternative organization of the world' (Stewart 1978: 166). Nonsense, then, can take us across cultural and cognitive fields, forcing us to confront the *other*, and his/her methods of organization. If the form and logic of print textuality began with books for 'little boys' (i.e., Ramus's textbooks), then the model for an electronic textuality might also come from books for children – nonsense books, that is. And not only from children's books, but from their video games and television shows as well.

Figure/Ground 3: Digital Media

Just as nonsense relies upon the predictability of sense for its existence, sense relies upon nonsense as a way of explaining away 'any mysterious gaps in our systems of order' (Stewart 1978: 15). Along with 'Fate, Chance, Accident, Miscellaneous, and even *etc.*,' nonsense provides a discursive space for storing the remainder[11] of language (ibid.). Susan Stewart characterizes nonsense as a strikingly intertextual mode of discourse, one which cannot occur without transgression, without contraband, without a little help of the *bricoleur*'s hand. To view nonsense in this way is to view communication as a constant interplay of 'universes of discourse' which are incessantly 'involved in borrowing from one another and transforming one another at every step as they are employed in an ongoing social process' (ibid.). This model of social intercourse is, of course, only a mouse click away from those models set forth by Barthes, Foucault, Kittler et al. as examined in the previous chapters. Stewart's intertextual model also has obvious affinities with hypertext, which, in its protean form, radically embodies many concepts of Continental theory, especially the notion of intertextuality. The Web can facilitate a rapid shift between various modes of discourse and cognition, all within the same perceptual field. Hence, whereas poststructural theory, the surrealists, children, and nonsense literature may all act as models of how to invoke a figure/ground shift that will short-circuit the discourse of the Republic of Scholars, hypertext offers us a forum, a material space, in which we can build our own models.

While I do not wish to glorify hypertext as an emancipatory mode of communication, this chapter outlines a method of research suited for development on the Web, the 'new medium' that has made the greatest progress in infiltrating the discourse of the Republic of Scholars. Admittedly, the computer is the most far-reaching new media tool in education, but it is not the only electronic tool that influences learning. Television, video games, even cell phones – marginal electronic media from a scholarly point of view – all play a part in education, even though they may not be an integral element of the classroom experience. Whereas Katherine Hayles rightly calls for an increased emphasis on material-specific critique, I am calling for an increase in material-specific pedagogy, starting with the materiality of the Web.

In *The Electronic Word*, Richard Lanham provides an in-depth examination of the figure/ground relationship that is possible in a graphic-rich computer environment. Although Lanham spends a great deal of his energy selling his own rhetorical model of hypertext at the expense of most other hypertext theorists, he goes beyond the typical musings on the convergence of hypertext and critical theory, and looks instead at how technology can enhance critical methodology. The AT/THROUGH binary is at the heart of Lanham's theorization:

> Such an oscillation between looking AT the expressive surface and THROUGH it seems to me the most powerful aesthetic attribute of electronic text. Print wants the gaze to remain THROUGH and unselfconscious all the time. Lichtenstein's *Magnifying Glass*, like the electronic screen, insists on the continual oscillation between unselfconscious expression and self-conscious design. (1993: 43)

Lanhman suggests that the role of scholars will change as they gain greater awareness of, and abilities in, desktop publishing tools that facilitate this oscillation:

So used are we to thinking black-and-white, continuous printed prose the norm
of conceptual utterance, that it has taken a series of theoretical attacks and technological metamorphoses to make us see it for what it is: an act of extraordinary
stylization, of remarkable, expressive self-denial. The lesson has been taught by
theorists from Marinetti to Burke and Derrida, and by personal computers
which restore to the reader ranges of expressivity – graphics, fonts, typography,
layout, color – that the prose stylist has abjured. (1993: 9)

Despite his acute observations on the affinities between hypertext and
avant-garde art, poststructuralism, concrete poetry, etc., Lanham does not
look to them as exemplars for new discursive methodologies. Instead, his
goal is to use new media to renew (digitize) the methodologies of classical
rhetoric. And since his ultimate hope is to 'redeem' 'the deepest and most
fundamental currents of Western education' (xii), Lanham parts ways with
those who are seeking for other channels that will lead to the invention of a
new academic apparatus. Lichtenstein's *Magnifying Glass*, which Lanham
discusses in his work, is reproduced here not only as a reminder for scholars
to look at the materiality of their work, but also as a reminder of the avant-
garde's tendency to critique – or radically embrace – technological culture,
and to invent new methodologies for resisting established social structures.

What Lanham neglects to consider is that hypertext may be used not only
as a sort of light switch between the classical, academic binary of rhetoric vs.
philosophy, but also as a multivalent switch, or *rheostat*, if you will, for toggling between cultural, epistemological, autobiographical, political, and historical categories. Hypertext, then, should not be considered as a digital on/
off switch for managing the components of classical scholarly discourse, but
as a forum for managing a much more complex, multivocal mode of discourse in which figure and ground, text and image, self and other, shift continuously. It may be useful here to leave behind the binary, *light-switch model*
of electronic writing and consider another model, that of Gregory Ulmer's
argumentative 'tuning knobs.' In his search for 'an alternative rhetoric, a
way out of the traditional prison of sequential exposition and logical argument' (Ray 1995: 82), Robert Ray draws on this more complex model:

We might think about the avant-garde practice that I have proposed as a means
of redeploying the three rhetorical principles of organization: narration, exposition, and poetics. The traditional allocation, of course, assigns narration to the
novel, exposition to the essay, and poetics to the poem, an arrangement ensuring
that each of the traditional forms will be structured around a dominant mode.
The avant-garde, on the other hand, demonstrates that an author producing a
text always finds himself like someone playing a video game, provided with
three knobs, labeled *narrative, expository, poetic*. At any point during the text's creation, he can adjust the balance (as one would adjust a television's colors),
thereby increasing (or reducing) the level of *any* of the three. From this perspec-

4.4 Roy Lichtenstein, *Magnifying Glass*, 1963.

tive, many avant-garde works begin to seem less strange: John Cage's lectures, after all, are only essays with the expository knob turned down and the narrative turned up; *Nadja* is merely a novel which increases exposition and poetics at the expense of narration. (1995: 200)

Although, in this excerpt, Ray confines the power of the tuning knobs to the properties of rhetorical form, this model seems equally appropriate for describing a mode of expression in which a variety of discourses interact, progress, and recede in a continuous shifting of figure and ground. If, along-side the knobs for narration, exposition, and poetics, we include knobs for politics, popular culture, theory, autobiography, etc., then we have indeed built a machine (a graphic equalizer?) capable of generating a mode of academic discourse more suitable to a culture of computing.

Figure/Ground 4: 1\0

The remainder of this chapter is devoted to the dissection of a Web project entitled *1\0*, which I completed in 1997 while sitting in on a graduate seminar conducted by Gregory Ulmer at the University of Florida. *1\0* is the first hypertextual experiment I completed in which I recognize traces of hypericonomy. The methodology employed in the project, which is a modification of Ulmer's 'mystory' concept, is a form of relay, handed to me by the various theorists, artists, and critics already mentioned in this book, including, of course, Gregory Ulmer. While *1\0* itself is certainly not a model of hypericonomy, it serves here as a case study in how to approach the invention of a new poetics in a classroom experiment. Here, I am the student assigned to assemble a mystory, and Ulmer is the instructor. In the next chapter, I am the instructor, and the students are electronic critique majors at the University of Detroit Mercy, grappling with hypericonomy.

The initial window, or home page, for *1\0* is emblematic of the entire project. This page consists of a large *1* and *0*, the hypericon of all things digital (now a recognizable cliché), pulsating on a background of thousands of ones and zeros combined randomly in a mesh of visual noise. The large *1* and *0* flicker incessantly, each digit changing from white to black, black to white, continuously. The viewer has a choice of clicking on either the *1*, the *0*, or the slash which separates them, and as in any hypertext, the choice determines what the viewer sees next. In this case, what the viewer sees next is not only an abyssal continuation of the 1\0 leitmotif, but a pictorial exploration of the binary of black and white across a series of discursive fields. While I knew that the black/white binary would be central to the project from the beginning, the 1\0 binary did not emerge until I had begun gathering all the materials for the project. What the hypertext amounted to, in essence, was an exercise in pattern recognition.

I have already described this strategy of *exploding the binary* in the semiotic square as it was employed by Rosalind Krauss to explore the problematic coupling of figure and ground. As in Krauss's project, *1\0* makes use of the semiotic square early on; but it does so in order to explore a more personal and social problem, that of racial tension. The semiotic square, however, fails miserably to solve the problem in this case, and only leads to a further complexification. If, in *1\0*, the semiotic square seems to provide no solution to the problem, no truly acceptable third term, it is because the goal of *1\0* is not to find a solution in the simple implementation of a graph, but to find a more complex, graphic means of embodying the problem. The idea is that by pic-

turing the problem from a series of discursive perspectives, a more comprehensive understanding of the issue may be achieved along the way. The
solution, then, is in the journey, not in the destination; it is in the creation of
a method, not in the application of one.

The semiotic square, employed on its own, is a much too rigid and positiv-
ist apparatus. For this reason, *1\0* relies heavily on a more pliable apparatus
known as the 'choral square.' The choral square, which first appears in
Ulmer's *Heuretics*, is a descendant of Plato's notion of *chora*, which was picked
up by Jacques Derrida. Like the mnemonic strategy of classical rhetoric or
oratory, chorography relies upon the generative potential of a specific place.
In Ulmer's chorography, the subject provides the place of invention, with the
intention of generating a poetics. The term *place* here is somewhat inadequate,
however, since it actually refers to the space of a quadripode graph which
Ulmer calls the *popcycle*, and within which the chorographer (or mystorian)
plots him/herself by filling in the following coordinates or slots: 'Family,
Entertainment, School, Discipline. Each of these institutions has its own discourse, including a matrix of logic, genres, modes, and forms relevant to its
function in the society' (Ulmer 1994a: 195). This description of the choral
square may sound somewhat cryptic at the onset (it certainly seemed so to
Ulmer's students – although this is part of his heuretic strategy), so it may be
better to follow Rosalind Krauss's wise words about dealing with a graph:
'it's both less tiresome and clearer just to show it' (1994: 13). During the brain-
storming phase of *1\0*, I filled in the slots of the choral square in the following
manner:

Family: recollection of an incident at a Caribbean Festival in which my sister
was verbally assaulted for supposedly making a racist comment, and I
was physically assaulted while a black friend of mine stood by, pretend-
ing not to know me.
Entertainment: the *Our Gang* or *Little Rascals* series produced at Hal Roach
Studios and at Metro Goldwyn Meyer, and especially the Buckwheat character.
School: images of slavery and torture recollected from childhood schooling
in which the film *Roots* and the story of Christ's Crucifixion played a
major role.
Discipline: the composite art of William Blake and the Blakean school of
Romantic criticism.

Evidently, these categories cross at various points. For example, the *Roots* film
that I saw in grade school could certainly be slotted into the 'Entertainment'
category, and the William Blake material could be categorized as 'School'
rather than 'Discipline.' What really matters for the sake of mystory, however,
is that the categories are filled in before the project actually begins, and they

are pursued faithfully as if they formed a set of rules for the deployment of the project. If, indeed, some of the categories cross conspicuously (for example, in all my memories of watching the Little Rascals, my brother is watching with me – a crossing of the 'Family' and 'Entertainment' categories), it is only because these discursive categories *always* cross at one point or another, in a more or less obvious way. The usefulness of the choral square, and of mystory in general, is that it allows us to see the cross-breeding of discourses, something that usually remains hidden or suppressed in academic work.

The popcycle first appeared in Ulmer's *Teletheory* as a set of guidelines employed in the creation of a mystory, a new critical genre which adds autobiography and pop culture to the scholarly mix. The categories of the popcycle have undergone a few transformations over the course of Ulmer's corpus, so that it is possible, I believe, to take certain liberties with it. This is where the relay toward a new poetics begins. We might, as I do in the next chapter, for example, replace the slots above with the categories of 'Personal Primal Scene,' 'Pop Culture Object,' 'Object of Study,' and 'History.' What remains essential in any case is that: (a) the academic category is forced to collide with other influential aspects of an individual's life; and (b) the categories are staged around the resolution of a specific problem.

The problem that I chose to bring into the choral square, as I have indicated, is that of black/white or racial tension. My intention was to explode this binary across a series of discursive fields. As I began gathering information – images, newspaper clippings, quotes, video – to fill in the slots, I noticed a recurring iconic pattern. Whether it was coincidence, chance, fate, or unconscious compulsion, the numbers *1* and *0* – along with a variety of thematic derivations such as the letters *I* and *O*, the circle and the line, the stick and the ball, a mouth exclaiming 'O!'[12] etc. – seemed to be present in one way or another in many of the images and text that I had chosen (it is present in this chapter as well in the mnemonic figure of the magnifying glass, which might be pictured as a zero atop a one, or an *O* atop an *I*). Without analysing this coincidence in depth, I decided to adhere to the pattern as a guide in selecting elements for the project. This method amounts to turning $1\backslash0$ into a hypericon, allowing it to encapsulate an entire episteme. It is this step toward creating an *economy of hypericons* that differentiates hypericonomy from mystory.

This resolution to *not analyse* the recurrent pictorial theme deserves further commentary here, since it is an essential element of mystory and of hypericonomy. If, according to Paul Feyerabend, 'by incorporation into a language of the future ... one must learn to argue with unexplained terms and to use sentences for which no clear rules of usage are as yet available' (1975: 256–7), then the commitment to deferring any in-depth analysis of one's thoughts and images during the *time of hypericonomising* must be considered as a seminal element of the method. Of course, for the hypericonomist, the language of the future includes unexplained pictures and graphs,

4.5 Ellis Nadler, *Detective with a Magnifying Glass*, 2005.

and not just 'terms' and 'sentences.' A hypericonomy, then, may be an exercise in nonsense writing, a testing ground for the production of a language
of the future. In Ulmer's terms, by filling in the slots of the popcycle, we are
'learning how to write an *intuition*, and this writing is what distinguishes
electronic logic (conduction) from the abductive (Baker Street) reasoning of
the detective' (1994a: 37).

   In hypericonomy, 'the intuitions are not left in the thinker's body but simulated in a machine, augmented by a prosthesis' (Ulmer 1994a: 37). Through
this process of simulated intuition, or 'artificial stupidity,' the writer, completely unaware, performs an outering of the ideological categories that structure his or her organization of knowledge (1994a: 38). Hypericonomy, then,
involves the invention of a new relation to knowledge itself, a techno-ideo-
logical relation which Ulmer calls a 'knowledge of enframing' (1989: 183).
Supported by the multi-noded network of hypertext, a sort of *pliable frame* to

be used in experimenting with this new relation to knowledge, the hypericonomist, toggling between ideological categories, comes to recognize the
extent to which 'the observer participates in the observation' (Ulmer 1989:
184). Hypericonomists are at once a sort of Marcel Duchamp and Marcel
Duchamp's ideal audience; through a praxis of *objet trouvé*, they are capable
of foregrounding the 'gray matter' of visual experience, and of subsequently
experiencing first-hand that 'the organization and classification of knowledge are *interested* activities' (Ulmer 1989: 184).

This deferred understanding, or 'artificial stupidity,' might be considered
as a form of *nachtraglichkeit*,[13] a psychoanalytic concept championed by Freud
and Lacan. *Nachtraglichkeit*, the translation of which is closer to 'deferred
action' than 'deferred understanding,' relates to the unknown (primal) scene
which remains buried in the analysand's unconscious as she relates a con-
scious recollection, working toward a primal scene. During this verbal recollection, this *time of understanding*, both analyst and analysand are in a position
of ignorance, and they must yield the initiative to language (or *lalangue*, in
Lacan's case) in order to come to terms with the primal scene. The point of recognition, then, can only take the form of a deferred understanding, an *under-
standing-too-late*, arrived at by means of a detour through the realm of
nonsense (puns, anagrams, macaronics, etc.). This journey through the
unconscious seems to run parallel with the passageway of the hypericonomist. When a hypericonomy such as *1\0* is finished, we are left with a veritable impression of its creator's unconscious (whether it be political, optical, or
psychic). But since this impression involves images from a shared culture,
history, and education, the implications go well beyond the psychic features
of an individual monad.

The project of rendering the unconscious in pictures is not a revolutionary
idea. One need only turn to the children's literature of the Grimm brothers,
for example, or, more explicitly, to the work of the surrealists, in order to
find an abundance of such renderings. The 'unveiling' of the unconscious, as
we know, is at the heart of the surrealist agenda, from the experimental film
of Dali and Buñuel, to the cryptic montages of Ernst. In *The Optical Unconscious*, Krauss goes into great detail about the visualization of the unconscious and the unconscious in visualization. According to Krauss, the work
of Ernst, Duchamp, and others helps illustrate the inextricability of desire,
the body, and the unconscious from the seeing eye:

> There is no way to concentrate on the threshold of vision, to capture something
> *en tournant la tête*, without siting vision in the body and positioning that body, in
> turn, within the grip of desire. Vision is then caught up within the meshes of
> projection and identification, within the specularity of substitution that is also a
> search for an origin lost. *Con*, as they say, *celui qui voit*. (1994: 140)

It is one thing for the surrealists to translate the unconscious into the symbolic world, to seduce an audience into an awareness of the unconscious; it is quite another to incite individuals into producing a representation of their own unconscious. 'Con, celui qui voit' is one thing; 'Con, celui qui se voit,' quite another.

In *Applied Grammatology*, Ulmer takes special note of Lacan's 'passion of ignorance,' his love for the '*sublime* of stupidity,' and his desire '*to instill it, to stimulate it, in the audience*' of his seminars (Lacan 1977: 19). Like Derrida, who urges us to yield the initiative to language, Lacan revels in the fact that 'I speak without knowing. I speak with my body, and that without knowing, I say thus always more than I know' (Lacan 1977: 108). Of greatest importance, here, is the fact that Lacan frequently employed images to instil this '*sublime* of stupidity' in his audience. On the cover of each volume of his seminars, for example, is a hypericonic image taken from classical painting – an 'organizing image of the discourse, not to be interpreted but to serve as a point of departure for working through a theoretical problem' (Ulmer 1989: 194). According to Ulmer, these images have a dual purpose: 'In the first place, alluding allegorically to the theme of the seminar, they provide a concrete point of reference for the discussion of certain principles ... The other function of the image is mnemonic, providing a reminder in association with which the year's work may be more readily recalled' (1989: 196). Each of the images in this psychic con game functions according to the delay of *nachtraglichkeit*, carrying Lacan's students through the *time of understanding*, creating expectation much in the same way that a frontispiece carries a child's imagination through the picture-barren pages of a book.[14] In Lacan's mnemonic technique, we have the precursor, the theoretical bud, of which hypericonomy is indeed the full bloom.

Of course, the hypericonomist does not work in complete darkness, or without any direction whatsoever. Although the destination of a hypericonomy may not be visible at the outset, we can set rules for how the content of such a project might be generated. In the case of *1\0*, the popcycle I selected provides the rules and spawns the initial content, while the *1\0* hypericon itself resonates in the abyss, generating associations and determining the general architecture of the project. This architecture, of course, is also determined by the technology within which it is enframed, and since, in this case, that technology is electronic, it is very difficult to offer a satisfactory impression of *1\0* in the confines of this printed text. As with a graph, in the case of a hypericonomy, it is 'both less tiresome and clearer just to show it' (Krauss 1994: 13). Since this chapter is not presented in the same medium as *1\0*, it is impossible to do justice to the project in any sufficient way; but still, it may be worthwhile to attempt a print-oriented reproduction of this project, if not to give the reader an impression of how *1\0* looks and works, then at least to demonstrate the impossibility of *translating* into the linear space of print this multinoded, non-sequential, electronic mode of discourse. The following list of nodes, then, transcribed from the *1\0* Web site, provides a virtual tour, a hypothetical example of how a single viewer might experience *1\0* as she browses through the project, following links at random.

Node 1 (fig. 4.6): Animated image of 1\0, alternating in black and white on a background of ones and zeros.

> The viewer clicks on the '1':

Node 2 (fig. 4.7): Greyscale digital reproduction from Blake's *Urizen*.

> The viewer clicks on the 'O!':

Node 3: Greyscale digital reproduction of 'Little Black Boy,' plate 1, copy I.

> The viewer clicks on the plate:

Node 4: Mrs Crabtree's brood, a film still taken from an episode of *The Little Rascals* in which Mrs Crabtree stands amidst her students.

> The viewer clicks on an image in the upper right-hand corner that represents two small details from the still: Mrs Crabtree's finger (1) and the circle around Petey the dog's eye (0):

Node 5: 'Cotten, the chimp,' a film still from an episode of *The Little Rascals*, comparing a black child to a chimpanzee.

> The viewer clicks on the word 'lamp':

Node 6 (fig. 4.8): Blake's ideographic writing. Images of circle, line, and light bulb, followed by animated morph of all three images. Commentary from W.J.T. Mitchell's *Picture Theory*.

> The viewer clicks on the word 'see':

Node 7: Greyscale digital reproduction of Blake's 'Little Black Boy,' plate 2, copies I and AA. Animation: images loop endlessly, one replacing the other in the same space at the left of the screen.

> The viewer clicks on the plate:

Node 8: 'Toby or Not' – image from Blake's *Jerusalem*. Text from memories of the author watching *Roots* as a child.

> The viewer clicks on the word 'denial':

Node 9: Little Black Boy / Caribbean Festival – left side from Blake's 'Little Black Boy'; right side from the author's personal experience.

> End of browsing.

A viewer might finish her exploration of the work with an account of my experience at a Caribbean Festival. Although *1\0* is supposed to confront the viewer with a centreless, non-sequential collection of texts and images, this experience at the Festival might be considered as the navel of the project since it describes the central problem, the primal scene in which the black/white binary is vividly foregrounded. Of course, in order to get to this autobiographical primal scene, I had to pass through the categories of 'Pop Culture' (the *Little Rascals* scenes), 'Discipline' (the Blake plates and commentary by W.J.T. Mitchell), and 'School' (the image of crucifixion and of slavery). Note

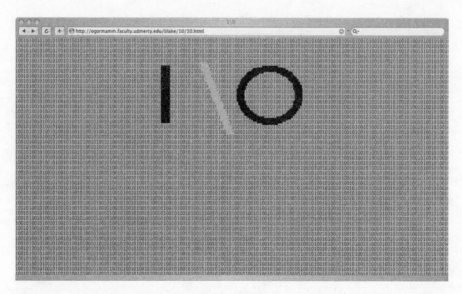

4.6 'Node 1,' opening page from *1\0*.

4.7 'Node 2,' interior page from *1\0*: William Blake, *The Book of Urizen*, Copy G, Plate 9, c. 1818.

But Blake's art does not just involve
pushing painting toward the
ideogrammatic realm of writing;

he also pushes alphabetic writing
toward the realm of pictorial values,
asking us to see his alphabetic forms
with our senses.

4.8 'Node 6,' interior page from *1\0*.

that I could have taken hundreds of paths to arrive at this page, and that the series of pages above only presents one possible sequence in which a viewer might browse through the project on the Web. The implications of this non-sequentiality are manifold; it could mean the difference, for example, between the viewer attributing this project to: (a) a racist artist; or (b) to an individual trying to subvert racist discourse.

Hypothetically, a Web surfer might arrive haphazardly on the Buckwheat page, and view this as the propagation of a racist stereotype common in American film and television: the submissive *pickaninny* who responds with an obedient 'Otay!' to the often outrageous commands of his white peers. On the other hand, viewers might see this page as humorous, reminding them of a harmless television program they watched as children. In either case, if the viewer clicks the links and continues browsing the project, her first impression might be completely eradicated, depending on the links that she chooses to follow and the amount of time and effort that she wishes to spend with the project. Hopefully, at the very least, the project would problematize or complexify any complacent first impressions.

In the end, however, it seems that discussing *1\0* from a viewer's perspective is a cumbersome, even tiresome, undertaking. There is a danger of explaining away a work which is intentionally enigmatic, and which is not meant to achieve any sort of closure. Rather than attempt to explain *1\0* or critique it as a work of art or of cultural criticism, it would be better to explore the experience of its creator during the process of its composition.

The ideographic figure of *O*, if you have the patience to circle it one more time, is how I have come to account for the general effect/affect of creating a hypericonomy. The project left me with a post-creation effect of shock, disorientation, and surprise – all of which can be summed up in the image of a jaw agape, a mouth stretched into the shape of a gasping *0*. This sense of disorientation makes it excruciatingly difficult to discuss a work like *1\0*, for even today it is still too close to me; it still fails to resolve the enigma which it embodies. I should also add that I now view it with a certain amount of nausea, based on the rudimentary quality of this early Web work. But at least the project gives my problem a space for resolution. This sense of shock and surprise might also be described as a sense of stupidity about the project and the problem it encapsulates. Could it be that to produce a hypericonomy of this sort is to place oneself in the presence of a sublime object?[15] An object which, in the Kantian/Derridean sense, invokes a 'violence done to the senses' (Derrida 1987: 130)? An object beyond the grasp of comprehension, beyond calculation and without end?

1\0 is merely one experiment, one controlled case study, in the attempt to design a new mode of scholarly discourse. I could discuss without end whether this sublime stupidity, this sense of shock or disorientation associated with such a project, might have something to do with the outering of an individual's unconscious, or with the displacement of the body and/or the memory into a machine. But this would be a step in the wrong direction at this stage of the experiment. Perhaps the best and only way for viewers to respond to an imagetext such as *1\0* is for them to create their own versions.

As I mentioned in the previous chapter, one does not have to be a skilled designer, artist, or iconologist to be a hypericonomist. The method reflects the current situation in which computer users approach their extremely complex and powerful machines as dilettantes. The sense of nausea that I feel when confronting *1\0* today has to do with the fact that I am confronting my own amateurism in 1996, my own lack of skill with Web design. But this lack of skill was pervasive on the Web at the time, and my site might be exemplary of the design style that characterized much of the Web in its early days. The point of underscoring this design issue is to demonstrate that, with the rapid and incessant changes in software and hardware manufacturing, the best way to approach digital media pedagogy may well be to train students in the art of 'well-informed dilettantism.' This is why William Blake, a poet, painter, philosopher, printmaker, and visionary, serves as an excellent exemplar for students in the humanities today. In the next chapter, I will approach the problem of designing a curriculum geared toward the educational formation of well-informed dilettantes, or digital intellectuals.

5. FROM ÉCRITURE TO E-CRIT:
On Postmodern Curriculum

Interdisciplinarity is not the calm of an easy security; it begins effectively *(as opposed to the mere expression of a pious wish) when the solidarity of the old disciplines breaks down.*

– Roland Barthes, *Image, Music, Text*, 155

Language of the Future

What would happen if students started producing, without solicitation, mystories, or even hypericonomies, for their professors? Could students get by with the vague excuse that they are 'writing in a language of the future,' and that they are therefore not obligated to be coherent? Could they claim that they are not subject to print literacy, and choose instead to produce something more in line with electracy? How would the instructor respond? Most likely, I suppose, by failing the students, or by asking them to resubmit their assignments in essay form, with paragraphs, page numbers, and references. I would not begrudge any instructor for reacting in this way, but I would call for a little more tolerance toward experimentation.

Hypericonomy is not a discursive tool designed to replace the academic essay. Instead, I hope the reader now understands that it is a hypothetical method for testing how scholarship might be transformed by new media and new theories of discourse. In other words, a language of the future is just that: a language to provoke thought about the future of discourse. A language of the future is impossible to imagine except in reference to a language of the present. Hypericonomy is not about immediately throwing out our current discursive practices, but about provoking change and inventing transitional, even provisional, strategies that bridge the gap between print-centric and computer-centric practices. Therefore, I would indeed like to see students submit hypericonomies rather than essays, but primarily for the sake of questioning the effectiveness and appropriateness of the conventional scholarly apparatus. As my students are often frustrated to discover, a hypericonomy must often be justified by means of an explanatory, print-centric essay. This is evidence that what I am proposing here is not the end of print or of linear writing, but the end of the print apparatus's stranglehold on higher education.

When I refer to 'my students,' I mean explicitly students in the Electronic Critique Program (E-Crit) at the University of Detroit Mercy (http://www.e-crit.com). One goal of this chapter is to demonstrate how the same theories and technologies that inform hypericonomy can also be applied to the creation of new curriculum. While hypericonomy challenges the discursive practices of traditional scholarship on a micro level, Electronic Critique confronts the larger discursive practices of the academic apparatus, namely the division of scholarship into compartmentalized disciplines, the persistent tendency toward specialization, the devaluation of the humanities, and the hierarchical relationship between student and instructor. Before moving into a precise discussion of curriculum, however, I would like to revisit hypericonomy once again, and describe a class assignment that can be used as a pedagogical relay for other instructors. As I have already made clear, it is not my intention to define an exact methodology, but to call for the invention of alternative discursive strategies. Therefore, the assignment that is described in this chapter is not meant to pin down hypericonomy, but to demonstrate one way in which hypericonomy might be interpreted, and how it might be implemented as an assignment that requires students to consider the 'metastructure' of the academic apparatus. The assignment, I hope, demonstrates how discursive innovation and curricular reform can go hand in hand.

The 4fold Vision

I first introduced an assignment called 'The 4fold Vision' to students in a survey of British literature class at the University of Florida in 1996. The majority of the class were first-year students in degree programs other than English, and they were surprised to be doing HTML coding in an English class. They were even more surprised to discover that their final assignment was not a three-hour exam or a ten-page essay, but an experimental hypertext project that required them to create imagetexts, drawing on William Blake as a design exemplar. When introduced to the assignment, several students – mainly the liberal arts students – were uneasy with the fact that they had to let go of conventional academic discourse. Other students, the ones who were not bewildered by the fact that their English class was located in a computer lab, liked the fact that they could avoid the drudgery of writing an

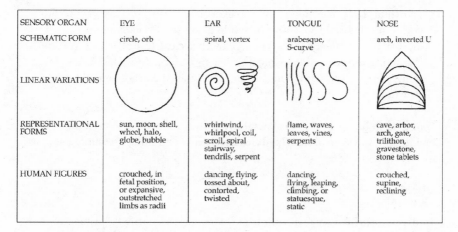

SENSORY ORGAN	EYE	EAR	TONGUE	NOSE
SCHEMATIC FORM	circle, orb	spiral, vortex	arabesque, S-curve	arch, inverted U
LINEAR VARIATIONS				
REPRESENTATIONAL FORMS	sun, moon, shell, wheel, halo, globe, bubble	whirlwind, whirlpool, coil, scroll, spiral stairway, tendrils, serpent	flame, waves, leaves, vines, serpents	cave, arbor, arch, gate, trilithon, gravestone, stone tablets
HUMAN FIGURES	crouched, in fetal position, or expansive, outstretched limbs as radii	dancing, flying, tossed about, contorted, twisted	dancing, flying, leaping, climbing, or statuesque, static	crouched, supine, reclining

5.1 W.J.T. Mitchell, 'William Blake's Pictorial Schemata.'

essay or an exam that they would most likely forget within a week of its completion.

Instructions for the 4fold Vision assignment were as follows:

THE 4FOLD VISION

If pictures are like sensory openings or perceptual structures, then looking at them is like putting on a new pair of spectacles or (more precisely) like opening your eyes. In other words, Blake's style, like that of any great artist, affects our vision: we start seeing vortices and arches and wave forms everywhere, in and out of Blake's pictures, just as we learn to see dark interiors from Rembrandt and storms from Turner.

– W.J.T. Mitchell, *Blake's Composite Art*

In the art of William Blake, the number **4** seems to dominate as a schematic element of organization – in other words, Blake often organizes characters, objects, and concepts/ideas into fourfold structures. The list of these quaternaries is so extensive that in *A Blake Dictionary*, S. Foster Damon is able to identify 26 Fourfold Correspondences in *Jerusalem* alone. Some examples are: Urthona, Luvah, Urizen and Tharmas (The Four Zoas); Sun, Moon, Stars, Earth (the four worlds); Imagination, Emotions, Reason, Senses (four divisions of man), and so on.

W.J.T. Mitchell picks up on this fourfoldness in *Blake's Composite Art* and draws on it as a tool for investigating Blake's pictorial style. Mitchell identifies a pictorial schemata in Blake's art, a fourfold vision which functions in three ways:

In formal terms, then, the function of Blake's schematic forms is to give structural consistency to his style; in expressive terms, it is his way of conveying his 'Fourfold Vision' – the world as sensed through all the gates of the body, not merely the eyes; and in rhetorical terms, it is a way of improving the sensual enjoyment of his spectators, designing visual illusions which continually demand and imply all the other senses in their structures.

Your goal in this project is to generate your own fourfold vision on the WWW by filling in the slots of the **4Fold Schema** below and linking them together as hypertext pages or *nodes*.

Directions

1) **Identify a *primal scene* in your life.** This is not necessarily *the* primal scene of Freudian fame (the one in which a child observes his parents engaged in sexual intercourse). Rather, as discussed in class, this primal scene is a single moment in your life in which you experienced intense confusion and internal conflict. The best scene is one taken from childhood memories, but you may also draw on a more recent scene as long as, in both cases, it is a scene charged with intense emotional conflict. Write about the scene as descriptively as possible, trying to recall the exact setting, the mood, small details, etc.
2) **Once you have chosen your primal scene, you will try to identify it with one of Blake's etchings from either *The Marriage of Heaven and Hell* or *Songs of Innocence and Experience*.** You don't have to justify your decision immediately, therefore, you may choose according to **instinct**. What plate appeals to you visually? What's your favorite? The connection to your primal scene will come later when you concentrate more closely on the **pictorial** elements of the plate in order to decide why it is like your primal scene.
3) **When you have identified the primal scene and chosen the plate, look for a pictorial element from Blake's schemata in both the primal scene and in the plate you have chosen** (i.e., a circle, an arch, a vortex, etc.). You will draw on that schematic shape as a thread that will link together your hypertext project.
4) **Once you have identified the scene, the Song, and the shape, allow these elements to 'explode' by spreading them across the 4fold Schema pictured below.** Fill in the slots of the schema, using your *primal scene* and your *primal shape* for guidance. The slots may be filled by using either images or texts. For example, you might want to use an image to fill the **History** slot, and a text to fill in **Education**. Or you may want to create more than one page for each of the slots, combining images and text. Some pages may be image only, some text only, and some a combination of the two. In selecting texts and images, you should consult the books and articles that we have studied in class, but you may also draw from other sources (i.e., television, magazines, Web sites, etc.) as long as they fulfill the requirements of the slot.

The 4Fold Schema

Personal	Historical	Pop Cultural	Educational
– primal scene	– specific moment – social conflict – race, gender, class	– favorite song, tv episode, film scene, etc. (keep it compact)	– one theory, concept, philosophy, etc.

5) Organize all of these elements into a hyperlinked project, paying close attention to your method of linking. The manner in which you combine these elements is up to you. Feel free to link to sites outside of your project as well (i.e., sites related to your 4Fold vision which appear elsewhere on the WWW). What you are looking for is coincidences between the various slots: textual puns, visual puns, underlying themes, etc. In this project, you shouldn't try to explain what themes you have discovered – show them by using links and other Web design elements (tables, frames, mouseover images, etc.).

The project will be graded according to the following categories:
50% Conception and Execution: Does the author understand the project, and has s/he attempted to fill in all of the required slots? Does the author express him/herself clearly in the portions that s/he has composed him/herself? Are there writing problems (grammar, spelling, diction, etc.) that obscure the author's message?
50% Design: Has the author taken steps to include both images and texts? Has s/he attempted to draw on the graphic elements available in Web page design (i.e., backgrounds, colors, fonts, images, alignment, tables, etc.), not just as ornamentation, but as elements of significant meaning? Is the text legible (not hidden behind graphics or written in a color that melts into the background)? Do the links provide multiple selections on each page and multiple pathways through the work?

– END OF ASSIGNMENT –

When I assigned the 4fold Vision project to first-year students at the University of Florida, the reaction was one of bewilderment. While the directions are extremely detailed, they are not specific about what the final project will look like. Most students understand what an essay 'looks like,' but how could they predict the outcome of a 4fold Vision? This lack of a model is essential since it forces students to craft their own form of visual rhetoric. In this way, the project requires students to engage more with heuretics (invention) than with hermeneutics (interpretation). The assignment does indeed require students to interpret texts (those of Blake and of the critical theorists covered in class), but it does not ask them to simply regurgitate what they have read. Instead, it asks them to use the texts as instructions in the invention of a new mode of discourse. The students were not writing about Blake, but *with* Blake, drawing on his radical dialectics and his image-texts as problem-solving tools. I was pleased with the results of the assignment in my University of Florida class, but it was not until I assigned the 4fold Vision to E-Crit students that I understood its greater potential.

In hindsight, there were problems with the way I implemented the 4fold Vision in my University of Florida class. First of all, because this was a final assignment, students did not have adequate time to reflect on their work. Additionally, I also failed to integrate an explanatory requirement into the assignment, which would have obligated students to justify their work in terms of the theories and texts covered in class. Finally, and most importantly, I was unable to question the students about whether or not this assignment had an impact on the work they completed in other courses; this is the ideal test of the effectiveness of teaching 'a language of the future,' which is supposed to be contagious, or even viral. Ideally, students who complete an assignment like the 4fold Vision should start being more critical of the research methodologies employed in their other classes. This is the first step toward turning a micro-discourse into a macro-discourse.

I did not make the same mistakes the first time I implemented the assignment to students of electronic critique at the University of Detroit Mercy. Rather than attempt to reproduce a 4fold Vision here, I have provided a sample text that one student, Amy Ruud, wrote in justification of her project. I include the text in full here since it captures the spirit of the 4fold Vision in a print-centric format, without providing some sort of model that might taint its heuretic potential for those who might implement the 4fold in class:

There's No Point, It's a Circle

I don't feel that I need to explain my art to you, Warren.
– A.J., Empire Records

Is it possible to be completely objective? To write an essay without any personal feelings or emotions? To hide yourself from your work? No. The truth is we all have feelings and emotions and experiences that affect everything we do whether we like it or not. The problem is that some don't like it, specifically, the academic apparatus doesn't like it. So should students be forced to forget everything that has ever happened them, to forget everything that they feel in order to write a paper? Instead of changing the student, let's change the apparatus.

The 4 Fold Vision is doing just that. But it is taking it a few steps further. It allows the students to take four parts of their lives, put them side by side, and make connections. In this case the four parts are: a primal scene or personal experience, a piece of history, a pop culture reference, and something academic. With these 4 parts the student is then to make connections and to apply those connections to a plate by William Blake.

Why William Blake? Because Blake used a certain schemata, shapes and symbols that are used throughout his work. The second part of the assignment was to find a common schema throughout our four parts and the Blake Plate and turn them into an animated gif, a slide show of pictures.

My 4 Fold was made up of my primal scene, when my friend Danny had a brain tumor discovered at the age of 8; my piece of history, when the Berlin Wall fell; my pop culture reference, the end of the film *Dogma*; and my academic reference, Jean Baudrillard. I then choose William Blake's *Visions from the Daughters of Albion*. The second part of the assignment was to create the animated gif. The shape I saw throughout my parts was a circle. I used the sun from Blake's Plate and connected that to the shape of the brain and of a tumor, to the 'O' in both *Dogma* and God, to a cylindrical shape on the Berlin wall that shows two hammers, and to the 'O' throughout a passage by Baudrillard.

So what is the point to the 4 Fold Vision? Well, my 4 Fold has no point, it is all circles. What I did right there is the point. Marshall McLuhan in his book, *The Medium is the Massage*, says, 'Learning, the educational process, has long been associated only with the glum. We speak of the "serious" student. Our time presents a unique opportunity for learning by means of humor – a perceptive or incisive joke can be more meaningful than platitude lying between two covers (10).' What McLuhan is talking about is puns. Finding connections between and among the different parts of not only the 4 Fold but all aspects of education and life. By making puns, the connections come easier and sometimes even clearer.

But it isn't just about puns. It can be about the third meaning as well. Roland Barthes explains the Third Meaning in his essay, 'The third meaning,' as the hidden meaning, specifically within film. But this third meaning can be found anywhere and it is only right for the viewer. It is something that is determined not by the film or the image itself, but by the viewer. Barthes says, 'The third meaning also seems to me greater than the pure, upright, secant, legal perpendicular of the narrative, it seems to open the field of meaning totally, that is infinitely ... The obtuse meaning appears to extend outside culture, knowledge, information ... It belongs to the family of pun, buffoonery, useless expenditure' (55). This is what the 4 Fold Vision accomplishes. It opens up the meaning of not only personal experiences, but educational ones as well. It also opens the meaning of the image of Blake, or any image for that matter.

The 4 Fold Vision is art and academia and personal experiences folding into one and justified by the connections made. It is changing the apparatus and the way academia behaves. It is not possible to completely remove oneself from their work and the 4 Fold Vision, by making its connections, proves why. No this is not the new 5 paragraph essay. It is an example of what can be done to change the way students learn so they won't have to change the way they live.

Amy's 'justification' of the 4fold project demonstrates the extent to which students might be asked to challenge the very structure and methodologies of the academic apparatus. Her description of the project as 'an example of what can be done to change the way students learn so they won't have to change the way they live' echoes Carl Raschke's proposition that 'the strange geometry of a hypertextual textuality means that the rules for the production of knowledge have to be invented as we move through the matrix of the new knowledge space' (2003: 78). It's important to note that Amy's project consisted not only of the hypertextual 4fold Vision, but also of an 'animated gif' that encapsulated the visual schema within her project. The animated GIF is important for two reasons: (1) it demonstrates that a project such as this can go beyond hypertext to include animation, video, immersive environments, etc.; and (2) Amy's ability to identify and give form to the repeating visual schema that held the project together indicates her knowledge of a new pictorial rhetoric, one that I have been calling hypericonomy. To look at it from another perspective, the 4fold Vision asks students to engage in a form of pattern recognition; it asks them to devise a method for organizing and producing knowledge that is suitable to a culture facing an onslaught of information, much of which is pictorial.

While the students' work inside the E-Crit Lab is indicative of the transformative potential of a heuretic pedagogy, the true test is when the students export a heuretic frame of mind into other classes. Students enrolled in the Electronic Critique Lab (ENL-491) at UDM are mostly E-Crit majors, taking a broad, interdisciplinary range of classes, which I will discuss below. ENL-491 requires students to bring their diverse disciplinary perspectives into the creation of collaborative projects that consider the impact of technology on culture. In the case of the 4fold Vision, as with all projects, the instructor is one of the collaborators – I was just as unaware as they were about how the 4fold Vision 'should look.' In assigning the project, I was not expecting to find a master model (a hypericonic equivalent to the perfect essay), but I was hoping that students might help me understand what it means to attempt to create a language of the future. Students were asked to comment about the assignment, and could request changes in the instructions, based on what they thought was appropriate for a digital culture assignment – hence the addition of the animated GIF. After all, it will increasingly be the case, I believe, that given the ever-growing availability of consumer-level media production software, students will be better versed in digital media than their professors. The students' questioning of the project itself (How is it unlike an essay? What does Blake have to do with digital culture? Why develop the project for the Web rather than Macromedia Director or Quick-

Time video?) not only changed the final outcome of the assignment, but also served as a force in shaping a large portion of the course content.

Critical Theory, Digital Media Studies, and the Curriculum of the Future

I would like to think that this pedagogical method is akin to what Carl A. Raschke calls 'transactional learning' (2003: 58). In *The Digital Revolution and the Coming of the Postmodern University* Raschke opposes interactivity (a common term in both pedagogy and new media development) to *transactivity,* which he sees as the pedagogical future of the 'postmodern university': 'Whereas interactivity can be a localized event in what is otherwise an authoritarian or highly structured and traditional learning space, transactivity involves the whole of the learning space, and the "learning culture" for that matter' (58). Borrowing a term put forth by John Gehl, editor and publisher of *Educom Review,* Raschke believes that the postmodern university is not about the learning infrastructure, but about its 'metastructure – a rethinking of the complete "why" and "wherefore" of learning' (58). Where I depart from Raschke, however, is that I don't believe this rethinking has to be dependent on distance education. Transactive learning may well be 'the term most appropriate to the learning space of a digital culture with the contours of a "world wide web"'; but the transactional learning space does not necessarily have to be a virtual space. I'm more interested in discovering how transactive learning can take place in a learning space where physical, human bodies are present.

Just as the invention of a new mode of academic discourse will not occur in the simple transferring of printed texts onto the Web, the transformation of university curriculum cannot take place by simply transferring print-centric pedagogy into distance education classes. As I have already discussed, in *Writing Machines,* Katherine Hayles attempts to transform the traditional academic monograph by remediating it according to the materiality of electronic media; the Electronic Critique Lab is an attempt to transform the traditional academic course by remediating it according to the same terms. According to Hayles, 'A critical practice that ignores materiality cuts itself off from the exuberant possibilities of all the unpredictable things that can happen when we as embodied creatures interact with the rich physicality of the world' (2002: 107). I would add that a pedagogical practice that ignores materiality (or that flattens human physicality into pixels on a screen) will not have the capacity to transform the academic apparatus in any humane way. Web-based distance education has already changed the way we understand the university, but it has simply transposed print-centric habits (with varied success) into a new learning space. I believe that the transformation of the academic apparatus is most likely to occur by means of physical agents that engage directly with the traditional material structures of learning, from the essay, to the classroom, to the entire campus itself.

I find it curious that Carl Raschke, a distinguished faculty member at the University of Denver, would not consider the way in which a program at his own institution, Digital Media Studies (DMS), is more 'postmodern' than the distance ed models he describes in his book. It is all the more strange since Raschke thanks Jeff Rutenbeck, director of DMS and president of the International Digital Media and Arts Association (IDMAA), in his acknowledgments. The DMS curriculum is a composite of the Departments of Computer Science, Fine Art, and Mass Communications. Students enrolled in DMS take live, embodied courses that range from 'Multimedia Authoring Tools' to 'Digital Noesis' (http://dms.du.edu). According to Rutenbeck, it is essential that DMS maintain its status as an interdisciplinary 'program,' rather than becoming a compartmentalized 'department' with its own faculty. This philosophy allows DMS to remain agile in the face of a protean computing culture. Rather than hiring faculty to teach in DMS, Rutenbeck uses revenue from the program's high enrolment to fund faculty positions in the various departments that support DMS, including Mass Communications, Fine Arts, and Computer Science. In this way, DMS not only supports its own curriculum, but also acts as a curricular innovator for several departments, helping them develop courses that stay on top of technological developments and theories. Perhaps what needs to be developed most of all, however, in programs such as DMS, is the study of metastructure. But, to date, this has been the specialty of English departments, where critical theory found a home a few decades ago and is now ready to migrate from its literary, print-oriented focus to the realm of digital artefacts.

While DMS originated in the Mass Communications Department at the University of Denver, other digital media programs in North America – the large majority of them graduate programs – have grown out of departments as diverse as Computer Science, Architecture, Film Studies, and Theatre. In the inaugural journal of the IDMAA, Conrad Gleber sums up this situation rather aptly:

> Across the academic scene in the United States and Europe to the Far East, digital media activities, articles, and new degree programs have been appearing in somewhat erratic fashion since the late '90s, at least. Most of these programs have lacked a clear discipline base. The areas of study often included multiple technologies including television and film, art, theatre, communication studies, architecture, computer science, journalism, technology programs, music, gaming, and others. (2004: 1)

While Gleber notes that digital media studies involves multiple technologies, from television to gaming, what's more important is that (a) he mentions the lack of 'a clear discipline base'; and (b) although he does mention art and theatre, he does not mention literature or the technology of print.

Gleber's list of technologies is, in spite of his claim otherwise, a list of academic disciplines, some old, some new, that make up digital media studies. The so-called lack of 'a clear discipline base' might be better described, then, as a multi- or transdisciplinary base, and in this sense, it is a lack to be cherished. While members of the IDMAA, myself included, strive for a better understanding of what constitutes a 'digital media and arts' curriculum, and examine the disciplinary origins of digital media studies, I would propose that the definition of such a curriculum should be left wide open for as long as possible. It is out of this baseless chaos that the 'postmodern university' might be crafted. It is also in this very arena that I foresee the evolution of literary/critical theory, a good reason to include English among the various departments out of which digital media studies might emerge.

As John Guillory has argued in *Cultural Capital*, the successful integration of critical theory into university curriculum is a result of its being introduced – as a sort of contraband – at the graduate level. 'The development of theory,' suggests Guillory, 'was always premised on the inviolability of the graduate seminar, the site of an autonomy not possible at the undergraduate level' (1993: 261). Guillory is referring specifically to the English graduate seminar here, and he notes that its autonomy may have more to do with the 'crisis in the humanities' (specifically literary studies) than it does with academic freedom:

> The indifference of university administrators to the graduate curriculum reflects less their respect for the traditional autonomy of the graduate teacher as it does an accurate estimation of the diminished significance of the literary curriculum in the context of the university's perceived social function, the perceived demand for the knowledge it disseminates. (1993: 261)

That 'perceived social function,' which is at the heart of Guillory's argument, is based on a techno-bureaucratic model; the university's role is to provide technically trained specialists with specific or 'rigorous' vocational skills. Subjects such as English, philosophy, and history are fine as a traditional supplement to a core curriculum, but they are perceived to have no market value in a techno-bureaucracy. As Guillory notes, '... the slot into which the humanities curriculum is confined is very small – as we know, the first two years of college study' (49). This amounts to nothing more than what Guillory calls a 'remedial'[1] attempt to infuse students with a form of cultural capital that has very little value outside of the few courses they are forced to take in the core curriculum. The way out of this crisis, Guillory suggests, is for

> progressive teachers to take back the humanities curriculum – all of it – as an integrated program of study. Such a program will be severely limited by the

narrow stratum of the educational system which it is forced to inhabit, but until we can begin to think and speak about education as a system of interrelated levels, these limits will continue to function subliminally, beyond analysis or intervention. (1993: 51)

As the surrealists reminded us, where some see crisis, others see opportunity. The 'off-the-radar' status of literary studies is capable of provoking severe self-pity in a traditional Romantics scholar. But to a Romantics scholar with an interest in critical theory and the materiality of visual communication, this state of neglect provides room for much-needed experimentation and revolution. In what Guillory might call a 'thought experiment,' the remainder of this chapter is a case study in an attempt to 'take back the humanities curriculum' under the guise of an integrative program of study that focuses on digital media.

Electronic Critique: A Case Study in Curricular Remediation

In 2002 the University of Detroit Mercy, a comprehensive Catholic university with a student body of about six thousand, launched an aggressive new marketing campaign to change its image. The slogan of the campaign, 'We Want Great Things for You,' accompanied by a picture of five faculty members surrounding a desk, was touted on billboards, Web sites, radio and television commercials, and in print materials, as a way of promoting the university's individualized care for students. What is most interesting about these campaign ads is not the imagery, however, but the 'goods' that they are offering for sale. While it seems that academic programs like Nursing, Engineering, Law, and even Architecture and Communications make for a good sales pitch, you would be hard-pressed to find the university basing a campaign on its 'diversified Philosophy curriculum,' or a 'forward-thinking English faculty.' Those faculty members are good for photos maybe (especially if they exude a Hollywoodized professorial aura), but the value of their intellectual labour just doesn't cut it in the enrolment marketplace. I include this terse media example as a tangible manifestation of what some have called the 'crisis in the humanities.'

As John Guillory has argued, for a short time, the crisis was allayed by 'rigorous' critical theory, which achieved a sort of 'rapprochement with the technobureaucratic constraints upon intellectual labor, symptomatically registered as a fetishization of "rigor"' (1993: xii). This leads Guillory to the conclusion that 'the moment of theory is determined, then, by a certain defunctioning of the literary curriculum, a crisis in the market value of its cultural capital occasioned by the emergence of a professional-managerial class which no longer requires the (primarily literary) cultural capital of the old bourgeoisie' (xii). If, as Terry Eagleton and others have argued, the 'moment of theory' has passed, and literary culture has not regained its value, where is English, let alone the other humanities disciplines, going to find an object of study suitably valuable – not to mention a methodology suitably rigorous – for the new bourgeoisie? The answer, I propose, lies in new media.

What I am suggesting is not that English departments should do away with the study of Great Books, but that they might consider, as John Frow does in *Marxism and Literary History*, redefining 'the traditional objects of literary knowledge, and in particular the forms of valorization of writing which have prevailed in most forms of literary study' (234). In response to Frow's call for a 'general poetics' that would take as its object not only literary texts but other non-canonical genres and forms, Guillory suggests that this has already been done in 'cultural studies.' However, as I have already discussed, cultural studies has only served to replicate 'the theoretical and hermeneutic paradigms of literary interpretation' (Guillory 1993: 265). The study of new media artefacts must coincide with the development of new media research methods.

It is 'nearly impossible,' Guillory suggests, 'to imagine what lies beyond the rhetoricism of literary theory, and hence beyond the problematic of literariness' (1993: 265). That impossibility, which is the very subject of this book, is also at the core of the crisis in humanities research, which defines itself primarily by means of print-based artefacts and practices in a world that is increasingly defining itself by means of digital media. It is time for the humanities to go digital (beyond archiving printed texts), and time for theory to go digital (beyond observing its own apotheosis in hypertext). This is the philosophy behind Electronic Critique.

I should note that the Electronic Critique Program, like the departments of English, philosophy, and history, is not included in any of the University of Detroit Mercy's broadcast advertisements. Although students in the program helped develop the university's Web site, and created its award-winning virtual tour in 2002, it would be financially risky for the institution to market such a program; in the words of one of our marketing directors, 'the title is a problem.' In fact, at a recent IDMAA meeting, I was asked to explain the title by a colleague who pointed out that the term 'electronic,' which encompasses everything from transistor radios to integrated circuits, is troublingly imprecise. Incessant queries about what the program is about have led me to consider changing the title to something more marketable like Digital Media Studies. But I have reconsidered each time, respecting the pleas of students in the program who see the title as absolutely appropriate, and also paying tribute to the program's founder, Hugh Culik, whose lingering influence reminds me that E-Crit is rooted in the study of *écriture*.

At the risk of endangering the current autonomy of the program, I will readily admit that very few individuals really know what E-Crit is all about, with the exception of students who majored in the program, most of whom thought they were going to get nothing more than an education in Web development, video, and interactive media. What they discover after a short while is that they are getting that and much more; they are getting a strong foundation from which to critique digital culture. From the perspective of university administrators, however, E-Crit remains a nebulous sort of computer art studio that encourages students to take on Web and video projects on campus (this has earned them a reputation as the institution's leading media developers). These projects allow the administrators to tout E-Crit as a cutting-edge program when questioned by alumni and suspicious senior faculty, but the conversation usually ends there.

My reason for divulging this 'under-the-radar' status of E-Crit is not to position the program as a fashionably subversive, leftist enclave (which it certainly is not), nor am I attempting to commit some sort of professional suicide. My goal is to make a point about the position of digital media, critical theory, and the humanities in the academic curriculum. Whereas English departments could sneak in critical theory on the basis of the indifference of administrators, pretty much any department can sneak in digital media on the basis of (a) the urgent desire of administrators to keep pace with perceived demands for high-tech programs; and (b) the administration's all-too-frequent lack of technical knowledge, which places it in the awkward position of trusting faculty members who claim to be making innovations in the curriculum. University administrators may have begun to catch on that critical theory is no longer as rigorous, scientific, or fashionable as they once thought, but digital media will continue to add perceived 'rigour' to the humanities for as long as our techno-bureaucratic managerial class maintains power. Now that critical theory seems to have exhausted itself on literary texts and practices, it is time for it to migrate elsewhere, into digital media, where it is perhaps even more relevant, suitable, and critical in the most urgent sense of the word. What's more, as a form of knowledge that seems to be inherent to the materiality of digital media, critical theory need not cloak itself in the graduate seminar. It can instead resonate at the core of an undergraduate curriculum, perhaps in computer proficiency exams or in first-year composition, where it can have a broader impact on the entire curricular structure of an institution.

My argument, then, is that critical theory and the humanities in general need digital media. But this goes hand in hand with the argument that digital media need critical theory and the humanities. In his mordant evaluation of the state of critical theory, Terry Eagleton suggests that

> cultural theory as we have it promises to grapple with some fundamental problems. But on the whole it fails to deliver. It has been shamefaced about morality and metaphysics, embarrassed about love, biology, religion and revolution,

largely silent about evil, reticent about death and suffering, dogmatic about essences, universals and foundations, and superficial about truth, objectivity and disinterestedness. (2003: 102)

In many ways, theory's failure has much in common with a culture that identifies with online dating, genetic engineering, and self-replication through increasingly sophisticated recordable media. When I propose that critical theory needs digital media and vice versa, I am proposing a curriculum that supports the thoughtful application of theory to the production of digital media artefacts, the creation of humane technologies and tech-related policies, and the investigation of the impact of technology on human being; or, to borrow Eagleton's shamelessly simple-minded words, I am proposing that educators can combine media and theory to 'find out how life can become more pleasant for more people' (2003: 5).

   As an exercise in imagining how such an idealist curriculum might look, I have provided below an outline of the current Electronic Critique curriculum, which is still in its formative stage, and may remain that way indefinitely. Once again, my goal here is not to sing the praises of what I perceive as some sort of romantically inspired 'curriculum of curriculums.' I am the first to admit that the E-Crit course of study has some weaknesses. As program director, I am realistic about the demands of the job market, and I am not interested in graduating disaffected dilettantes with a shallow but wide array of skills. With the philosophy of the program in place, the challenge is in maintaining flexibility without completely neglecting the demand of specialization that students will face after graduation. Currently, the program curriculum appears in the university catalogue as follows:

E-Crit Core (12 Credits)
All E-Crit Majors must complete the following four courses:
CIS 103 Web Productivity Tools
ENL 305 Freelance Writing: Print and Web
HIS 360 History of American Technology
PHL 140 Topics in Critical Thinking: Media

Disciplinary Concentration (18 Credits)
E-Crit is rooted in a traditional Liberal Arts education. Therefore, all majors must pursue a disciplinary concentration from a department in the College of Liberal Arts. Each Department will recommend courses suitable for E-Crit majors.

E-Crit Design Laboratory (12 Credits)
Students enroll in the E-Crit Lab four times.
ENL 491 E-Crit Design Lab

E-Crit Tracks (15 Credits from one of the tracks below)
Students in E-Crit must select from one of 2 specialized tracks – Programming OR Design – in order to develop an area of expertise related to information technology. Recommended courses are listed below. Substitutions may be made with the approval of the Program Director. In keeping with the cross-disciplinary commitment of E-Crit, majors are encouraged to combine these tracks with certificate programs in other Colleges (see below).

Programming Track (15 Credits)
CIS 201 Introduction to Programming
CIS 220 Programming for the Internet
CIS 281 Data Communications and Networks
CIS 305 Requirements and Design
Plus, choose one of the following: CIS 335 Interface Design, CIS 382 Database Design, CIS 460 Technologies for E-Commerce.

Design Track (15 Credits)
AR 116 Introduction to Computer Graphics (School of Architecture)
AR 216 Computer Design (School of Architecture)
AR 371 Graphic Design (School of Architecture)
Students in this track must complete at least two more design-related electives at the 300-400 level.

Digital Media Portfolio (3 Credits)
All students must complete the portfolio in their last term of study.
ECR 499 Digital Media Portfolio

Students in E-Crit take many of their courses in the areas of computer information systems, communications, and architecture, but they must also complete a disciplinary concentration in one liberal arts department, preferably in the humanities. While I will refrain from an extensive explanation of the evolution of this curriculum, I will point out some pertinent details regarding the two tracks. As a result of the university's folding of the Fine Arts Department, the design track, in its initial state, could only be completed by taking courses at a local college in our consortium (Marygrove College). This situation has changed as E-Crit achieved a more integrative relationship with the School of Architecture. But that relationship is beholden to a seemingly impervious architecture curriculum. In the same way, the imperviously 'rigorous' nature of the Computer Science Department has required the Programming Track to migrate toward the more agile Computer Information Systems Department. These inter-collegiate relationships are the long-term goal of the E-Crit curriculum, which seeks immediately to position a viral digital curriculum within the College of Liberal Arts, with the grandiose, long-term hope that it will have a humanities-oriented, transformative impact on all departments involved with the program.

Ideally, administrators of a program such as E-Crit or the University of Denver's DMS program would design a project-based, interdisciplinary curriculum based on current IT-enhanced courses, and continually foster the creation of new courses in other departments and possibly other colleges. In addition, students in the program should, through a bottom-up effect, help spur the transformation of pedagogical techniques and course design so that their education becomes more suitable to a digital culture. The point would not be just to help those departments 'go digital,' but to encourage the integration of critical thinking into all digital media courses.

It is important to bear in mind that, at the time of writing, the E-Crit Program was only five years old, and that the curriculum outlined here should be viewed as temporary and transitional. It is not meant to act as a model, but as a relay for curricular innovators. The next phase of the E-Crit curriculum involves the creation of new courses that are cross-listed in other colleges, thereby giving an added complexity to John Guillory's vision of an 'integrated program of study' in the humanities. For example, the Department of Electrical Engineering might offer a class in microcontroller programming that would involve students from both engineering and liberal arts in the creation of electronic devices suitable, for example, for a critical/ digital art installation. Another example would be a cross-listed course in architecture that involves students in the creation of 3-D interactive spaces that urge participants to experience the discrepancy between the infinity of cyberspace and the finitude of the human body. What the instructors of such courses must realize is that their goal is to act as interdisciplinary mediators capable of mobilizing diverse skill-sets in the achievement of a single goal. In many cases, the instructors will find themselves to be collaborators rather than leaders, having been outskilled by students with greater computing proficiency, or with a different specialized skill-set. What matters, however, is that instructors maintain the role of mediator and facilitator for the students, keeping them focused on the 'big picture' of their projects.

This admittedly idealized model seems to fall in line with the way in which Carl Raschke characterizes the 'hyperuniversity.' He does so by contrasting a 'traditional knowledge paradigm' to an 'emerging knowledge revolution,' which he characterizes as follows:

Nature of knowledge production: De-centralized;
Character of learning: Bottom-up, client-centered, outcomes-designed, task-oriented;
Structures of education: Customer-driven, standards-related;
Knowledge acquisition: Self-directed inquiry, certification programmes built around specific objectives, 'menu-driven' selection of curricular options;

Knowledge space: Socially distributed, gated by access technologies, democratic;
Criteria for 'expertise': Application of formal education to social knowledge, interdisciplinary facility, participation in broad, cultural 'knowledge base.' (2003: 21)

Here, Raschke has remediated the Web, re-purposing its characteristics toward the construction of a new knowledge paradigm. This is an excellent menu of ingredients for a postmodern university, but for those who see this as a desirable model, one question still remains: how do we get there? As Raschke indicates, 'The educational eschaton may not be as closely at hand as many have lately imagined. In fact, both the overpromise of technology by itself and the tenacity of the "roaring Nineties" are evident' (2003: 20–1). The 'dot.com' bust only serves to increase resistance to change in academia, but university administrators still recognize the powerful cultural capital of digital media, as evidenced in the persistence of distance education projects. But a legion of University of Pheonix's will certainly not spur a knowledge revolution. As I have already suggested, as prompted by Raschke, the key to revolution lies in reconsidering the university's metastructure; that is, the key is in challenging, from within, the university's print-centric, compartmentalized knowledge paradigm. For those who are fortunate enough to have the opportunity to create a new academic program, that challenge can take the shape of a large-scale, programmatic intervention. For others, the only viable option is at the level of individual discursive intervention. This, after all, is where the battle will ultimately be waged. Even those instructors who do not integrate technology into their courses, and who do not work in interdisciplinary programs, can still focus on teaching students about the 'metastructure' of their education, focusing on the role of discourse in shaping their respective disciplines.

E-Crit and *écriture*

This book begins with an epigraph in which David Harvey summarizes the philosophy of Michel Foucault: 'The only way open to eliminate the "fascism in our heads" is to explore and build upon the open qualities of human discourse, and thereby to intervene in the way knowledge is produced and constituted at the particular sites where a localized power-discourse prevails' (1989: 45). Whenever a colleague in another department complains about how one or more of 'my students' disrupted class by challenging his or her disciplinary method or *metanarrative* (this happened most recently when students questioned the ideological slant of a history-class textbook) I feel, in a muddle of relief and apprehension, that the revolution is still underway.

The term 'revolution' will quite possibly always remind me of Hugh Culik, the founder of Electronic Critique, who co-wrote the manifesto below, and who always ends his e-mail messages with the Marxist credo: 'for the revolu-tion.' As Culik indicates, E-Crit was formed out of a need for resistance, spe-cifically, resistance to 'the ideologies that make up electronic culture.' This may seem like an ironic statement coming from the founder of a program rooted in electronic culture, and indeed it is. E-Crit requires students and fac-ulty to take an ironic stance toward technology; to be 'in technology, but not of technology,' as a deceased colleague of ours once said. Educators and aca-demics who wish to see a revolution in academia might not consider them-selves products of the current technological apparatus, but they may turn to new technologies as a way of resisting its dehumanizing effects. For change to occur, they must, above all, work within the current apparatus, engaging with its very materiality on all levels.

While the notion of being 'in technology, but not of technology' is evidently informed by a Christian ethic (in fact, the quote is taken from Christian Koontz, a Sister of Mercy), it also echoes a postmodern or, more appropriately, a poststructuralist understanding of language. That is, poststructuralists write with the understanding that writing itself is an imperfect mode of com-munication. The playful metadiscourse of deconstruction – writing about writing – is rooted in a resistance to power structures that attempt to define absolute, objective meanings. While poststructuralists – Derrida, Barthes et al. – turned to *écriture* (playful writing that foregrounds the gaps in language, the impossibility of transparent communication) as a method of resisting the 'fascism in our heads,' Culik proposed E-Crit, an equally poststructural inter-vention, a curricular embodiment of poststructural thought:

e-crit #1: Resistance, Progress, and Praxis
by Hugh Culik and Nick Rombes

What else is there but resistance? No cultural formation is sacred. Isn't critique a form of resistance, and isn't that what E-crit is all about? To unmask / expose / and finally resist the ideologies that make up electronic culture while at the same time playing poker with the devil? How do we resist? Through interroga-tion and rebuilding as always. Perhaps at the end of the day there is much that we will accept, but only after resistance. That's why resistance is not the same as rejection. We don't mean rejection, we mean resistance. A dialectic that is con-tradiction – being against the thing you are for. The tension that comes from making the thing apologize for being what it is.

So how do we do it, practically? We start and end with the mapping that the-ory makes possible, because finally that is the free-est space there is. That in itself is resistance. We must never underestimate that. The rest is performance, simply an outgrowth of theory. Without the theory, performance is nothing more than fumbling in the dark.

What are the enemies of resistance? Expediency. Efficiency. Productivity. In their service, critical thought is lost. The forces upon us now: to show results, to chart enrollments, to take exit polls, to survey, to record, to measure. We must be careful that our resistance to this apparatus doesn't become the resistance of the 'losers' – that is, weak, lazy people also resist these things, and we are not them. So how to resist without becoming bitter, cynical, reactionary?

How, in other words, does resistance remain progressive? Perhaps we need to articulate the mutuality of the two. For resistance can easily become the hiding place for utopians/dystopians, and we are not them. We think the answer is simple: Resistance does not necessarily mean being 'against' electronic culture. Rather, resistance means forcing open the objects of the new culture and interrogating them. They are not 'special,' 'sacred,' or 'untouchable.' Nothing is.

And because they are the dominant objects of our culture now, it is our duty to resist them. Not one ounce of us believes that resistance is futile. Not one ounce. If you and we believe – and we think we do – that power is a constant that's merely redistributed in various disguises as the culture changes, then it's our duty to seek it out, expose it, and resist it wherever it may lie. For power rarely announces itself as such (how many Hitlers can there be in a century?).

Resistance is not futile because we say it's not.

This stereotypically bombastic manifesto seems to make a vague claim about what exactly it is resisting and why. But this is not a case of resistance for the sake of resistance. The frustration voiced here is the result of grappling with a university apparatus that has responded to new technologies by vacillating between (a) repressive traditionalism; and (b) blind enthusiasm. As is evident, this manifesto is written in the spirit of movements such as dadaism, futurism, and surrealism. Its purpose is to reclaim the political and revolutionary potential of the twentieth-century avant-garde, which, like poststructuralism itself, seems to have been lost, liquidated into a metaphor for computer technology. As Lev Manovich has suggested, 'One general effect of the digital revolution is that avant-garde aesthetic strategies came to be embedded in the commands and interface metaphors of computer software. In short, *the avant-garde became materialized in a computer*' (2000: 306–7).[2] Rather than turn the political and intellectual dynamics of poststructuralism or the avant-garde into a selection of menu items in a design program, E-Crit is an attempt to remotivate those dynamic strategies, and recouple them with their (now digitized) aesthetic strategies.

The problem with reproducing an entire curricular schema and reiterating philosophical manifestos, as I have started to do here, is that of falling into the trap of producing yet another metanarrative, another explanatory model.[3] Describing the Electronic Critique Program as some sort of 'ultimate postmodern academic program' – which is not my intention here – would be an exercise not only in hubris, but in futility. I will stress once again that the current E-Crit curriculum is a revision of a revision of the curriculum initially proposed by Hugh Culik and Nick Rombes when the program was founded in 1999, and it will continue to be revised. In addition, there is no guarantee that the E-Crit Program will still exist by the time this book is printed, which would turn this chapter into a nostalgic artefact. As a final statement on 'post-modern curriculum,' then, I will suggest that it must be as agile and ironic as the *écriture* of Barthes and Derrida.

A Final Note on Techno-Romantic Idealism

As a final supplement to the case study offered in this chapter, I have included a fragment from a document drafted by the University of Detroit Mercy's Future of Computing Committee in the winter of 2001. The committee consisted of faculty members from Electrical Engineering, Computer Science, Computer and Information Systems, Architecture, Communication Studies, Electronic Critique, and, upon my urging, English. The meetings of this committee led to the composition of a vision statement about the future of computing at the university, which was approved by the deans of the various colleges implicated, certified by the provost, and reviewed by an external committee of IT experts from various institutions around the country. The document, composed by myself, an English Department faculty member, and an electrical engineer, reflects the philosophy of Electronic Critique (although most committee members would never have realized this) and roots its vision in the production and dissemination of critical discourse. The crux of that vision is as follows:

> Students must understand and participate in the disciplinary, economic, and cultural dynamics that determine which types of technologies are considered valuable and which are not, and that determine which types of information are legitimated as knowledge, and which are discredited. They must be able to navigate a bombardment of complex textual, aural, and visual information that is often created to persuade them with rhetorical finesse. They must have the necessary critical frameworks to sift through that and to recognize the face of rhetorical persuasion in order to make informed professional, personal, and consumer decisions. In essence, students must not only be able to use computation and information technologies in creative and powerful ways, they must also be able to articulate the nature of the new forces shaping their society, and to demystify their assumptions – assumptions that often depict 'information,' 'knowledge,' and 'technology' as neutral, objective entities rather than as cultural constructs with social, economic, political, and ethical implications.

In spite of the strong rhetoric of critical thinking employed here, the efforts of the Future of Computing Committee did not achieve any recognizable impact whatsoever on the 'rigour'-driven curriculum at the institution. What it did accomplish, perhaps, is to increase the cynicism and weariness of a group of individuals who are sincerely interested in remediating higher education, but who are tired of having the materiality of their ideas confined to ink and paper.

In an e-mail message that I received after the Future of Computing vision had long been forgotten, one committee member (who has requested ano-nymity) aptly voiced the frustration of being trapped between the tradi-tional bourgeois ideology of academe and the techno-bureaucratic demands of the pervasive culture:

> Everything sounds good in the general meetings, promises are made, but when actual curricular changes need to be made, nameless department committees raise concerns and objections and we end up with very limited actual progress. In some cases the concerns were based on workload; where will we get the time to develop the new lecture material? In other cases, the objections arise from a commitment to legacy programs; 'we have always done it this way.' I do think, as I write this, that if institutional resources were made available for course releases, faculty would likely have been more willing and able to make some progress. However, there are other problems which are not easily addressed by a course release. In the EE [Electrical Engineering] program for example, our program is very tightly woven around the ABET [Accreditation Board for Engi-neering and Technology, Inc.] accreditation requirements with a suffocating series of assessment and evaluation reports being generated each semester to demonstrate compliance and 'continual improvement.' (2 June 2004)

Between the repressive constraints of 'legacy' and the techno-fetishistic demand for 'progress' levied by the ruling managerial class, curricular inno-vation has very little chance of leaving the confines of an idealistic vision statement. Even if the institution would support the creation of a new inter-collegiate digital media program, notes the anonymous faculty member, 'it would likely have to be a master's level program.' What's more, an innova-tive program can only be as strong as the institution that supports it, and can only succeed with institutional support – which is a great deal to ask when the program challenges the institutional structure that is in place.

The point of this final supplement is not to discourage even the most rig-orous of techno-romantics from dreaming of an integrative curriculum that will 'save the humanities.' Rather, my objective is to illuminate some of the difficulties that such individuals can expect to face in the process of materi-alizing their imaginary educational structures. It is no coincidence, perhaps, that as I compose this final chapter, the Electronic Critique headquarters seems to be migrating from the College of Liberal Arts to the School of Architecture. My hope, which should be read allegorically, is that this migra-tion reflects a long-awaited and hopefully long-term engagement between theory and materiality, and not a failure on the part of a humanities-based college to sustain the revolutionary demands of electronic critique.

NOTES

Introduction

1 In the semiotic battle over the term 'new media,' I have yet to find a satisfactory compromise. In *The Language of New Media*, Lev Manovich reserves the term for when 'graphics, moving images, sounds, shapes, spaces, and texts become computable, that is, simply sets of computer data. In short, media become new media' (25). I am more drawn, however, to the following credo of Lisa Gitelman and Geoffrey Pingree in *New Media, 1740–1915*: 'All media were once new media' (xii). This suggests that the term 'new media' is historically determined. While I use the term primarily in reference to electronic media, I also understand that contemporary, North American culture is not the first to encounter a material shift in technological modes of communication and representation.

2 For a more detailed look at academia's hypertextual fever for archiving, see my essay 'A Fever for Archiving: How Humanities Scholarship Works the Web,' in *Space and Culture* (Spring 2001).

3 In *Remediation*, Jay Bolter and Richard Grusin assert that 'no medium today, and certainly no single media event, seems to do its cultural work in isolation from other media, any more than it works in isolation from other social and economic forces. What is new about new media comes from the particular ways in which they refashion older media and the ways in which older media refashion themselves to answer the challenge of new media' (15).

1. The Canon, the Archive, and the Remainder

1 For a brilliant illustration of how the remainder might haunt a work of art, see Julian Barnes, *A History of the World in 10 1/2 Chapters*, chapter 5, part II. In this chapter, Barnes engages in a critique of Géricault's *Raft of the Medusa* by contemplating 'what he did not paint' (126). The result is a brilliant critique of totalized history, the Gorgon of all postmodern fiction.

2 Guillory suggests that the introduction of literary theory into the humanities curriculum is a product of the university's demand for 'rigor,' metrics, and calcula-
ble scientific methods. In Guillory's terms,

> The syllabus of theory has the oblique purpose of signifying a rapprochement
> with the technobureaucratic constraints upon intellectual labor, symptomati-
> cally registered as a fetishization of 'rigor.' The moment of theory is deter-
> mined, then, by a certain defunctioning of the literary curriculum, a crisis in the
> market value of its cultural capital occasioned by the emergence of a profes-
> sional-managerial class which no longer requires the (primary literary) cultural
> capital of the old bourgeoisie. (xii)

I argue below that digital archiving in the humanities is a symptom of the same
fetishization of rigour and devaluing of the cultural capital of both literary and
interpretive texts.

3 The essay in question was eventually featured at the *Romantic Circles* Web site,
under the following title: 'Picturing the Canon in an Electronic Age: Provisional
Treatment for Archive Fever' (http://www.rc.umd.edu/). The essay was later
published in print as 'A Fever for Archiving: How Humanities Scholarship
Works the Web,' in *Space and Culture* (Spring 2001).

4 Although the rhizome concept of Deleuze and Guattari can by no means be
summed up in a single endnote, their advice on how to write rhizomatically
might act as a striking introduction to their rhizomatic theory: 'Write to the nth
power, the n-1 power, write with slogans. Make rhizomes, not roots, never plant!
Don't sow, grow offshoots! Don't be one or multiple, be multiplicities! Run lines,
never plot a point! Speed turns the point into a line! Be quick, even when standing still! Line of chance, line of hips, line of flight. Don't bring out the General in
you! Don't have just ideas, just have an idea (Godard). Have short-term ideas.
Make maps, not photos or drawings' (1987: 24–5).

5 The term 'relevance' should not be taken lightly here, for it forms the core of an
increasingly influential communication theory – *the principle of relevance* – put forth
by Dan Sperber and Deidre Wilson. In an attempt to fill in the gaps left by linguists
and anthropologists from Saussure to Barthes, Sperber and Wilson suggest that
'the principal of relevance is enough on its own to account for the interaction of linguistic meaning and contextual factors in utterance interpretation' (1986: vii).

6 Drawing on Deleuze and Guattari's literal interpretation of 'body politic,' Lecercle insists that 'if there is such a thing as violence in language, the term must be
taken literally – not the violence of symbol, but the violence of intervention, of an
event the immateriality of which does not prevent it from having material effects,
effects not of metaphor but of metamorphosis' (1990: 227). In *Roots*, Kunta-Kinte's
reluctance to accept the slave name 'Toby,' and his subsequent torture for this
nominative rebellion, is an apt example of the literal violence of language: the
master's linguistic attempt to intervene in African history, and Kunta-Kinte's
resistance to this violent intervention.

7 'A rhizome has no beginning or end; it is always in the middle, between things, interbeing, *intermezzo*. The tree is filiation, but the rhizome is alliance, uniquely alliance. The tree imposes the verb "to be," but the fabric of the rhizome is the conjunction, "and ... and ... and ..." This conjunction carries enough force to shake and uproot the verb "to be." Where are you going? Where are you coming from? What are you heading for? These are totally useless questions' (1987: 25).

8 As Andrew Cooper and Michael Simpson suggest in 'The High-Tech Luddite of Lambeth: Blake's Eternal Hacking,'

> The welcome page [to the Blake Archive] bids us enter the feast and disport ourselves. But our freedom may be dearly bought, because this welcome immediately embroils us in a legal disquisition about what we may and may not copy from the glittering plethora of private property that constitutes the content of the Archive. (1999: 125)

In *Writing Machines*, Katherine Hayles recounts her ill-fated experience of criticizing the print-centric rhetoric of the Blake Archive at a conference of the North American Society for the Study of Romanticism. Her conclusion, that 'the literary community could no longer afford to treat text on screen as if it were print read in a vertical position' (43), was not very well received.

9 In an excellent response to the launching of the Web-based Romantic Chronology, Alan Liu expresses hope that a digital archive may achieve more than making literary texts more consumable:

> My own hope as a collaborator on this project is that a chronology at the present moment can indeed be constructively critical of the form that subjects it to the culture all around it. The trick is to see how such a chronology can make imaginable modes of knowledge that are other than the current, institutionally-dominant modes of giving consumers or students the goods. (Lin 2005)

By comparing the chronology to a typical pop-culture '10-best' list, Liu is underscoring the notion that digital archiving is indeed a symptom of the academic apparatus's techno-bureacratic outlook. His call for imagining alternative 'modes of knowledge' echoes the thesis of this book.

10 In this classic Carrollian instance of nonsense, the White Knight confuses Alice by differentiating between what 'the name of the song is called,' 'what the name is called,' 'what the name really is,' and 'what the song is called' (Carroll 1963: 306). This scene of infinite linguistic digression has been identified by many philosophers and critics as a perfect example of 'Frege's paradox.' In *The Logic of Sense*, Deleuze draws on this scene to demonstrate what he calls the *aliquid* nature of sense, which may be summed up (inadequately, of course) in the following proposition: 'I can never state the sense of what I'm saying. But on the other hand, I can always take the sense of what I say as the object of another proposition whose sense, in turn, I cannot state' (28). This proposition echoes, quite clearly, the White Knight's digressive discourse.

11 Admittedly, this is a vast oversimplification·of the ideological categorization of madness as treated by Foucault and others. See Michel Foucault, *Madness and Civilization: A History of Insanity in the Age of Reason*, trans. Richard Howard (New York: Vintage, 1985).

2. The Search for Exemplars

1 As Ethan Gilsdorf put it in 'Surrealism's Bittersweet End,' 'We've come a short way, baby, since Luis Bunuel and Dali's 1929 film *Un Chien Andalou* – we now have talking dogs in Taco Bell commercials' (*Chronicle of Higher Education*, 13 June 2003, p. B16).

2 It is impractical, perhaps impossible, to do justice to Foucault's unique and multi-faceted definition of *archaeology* in a single endnote. For this reason, I have settled for the following description of his archaeological practice – one which captures the concept of 'discourse networks' – and let the remaining definitions fall where they may: 'The horizon of archaeology, therefore, is not *a* science, *a* rationality, *a* mentality, *a* culture; it is a tangle of interpositivities whose limits and points of intersection cannot be fixed in a single operation. Archaeology is a comparative analysis that is not intended to reduce the diversity of discourses, and to outline the unity that must totalize them, but is intended to divide up their diversity into different figures. Archaeological comparison does not have a unifying, but a diversifying, effect' (1971: 159-60).

3 Kittler's republic of scholars is a prime example of what Carl A. Raschke identifies as the 'clerical' archetype of education. 'According to the clerical archetype, the goal of instruction is to inculcate in the students the kinds of beliefs, values, and moral practices that will demonstrate that they are, first, worthy of eternal salvation and, second, capable of living a virtuous and socially productive life' (2003: 54).

4 John Guillory alludes to this tradition in *Cultural Capital* when he notes the relationship between the literary canon and the scriptural canon: 'The concept of the canon names the traditional curriculum of literary texts by analogy to that body of writing historically characterized by an inherent logic of *closure* – the scriptural canon' (6). Tampering with the canon, then, or with other traditional academic structures, including scholarly discourse, may be viewed as a threat to religious practice and doctrine.

5 The following paragraph might serve as a definition of *heuretics*: 'As an "experimental" humanities, heuretics appropriates the history of the avant-garde as a liberal arts mode of research and experimentation ... Without relinquishing the presently established applications of theory in our disciplines (critique and hermeneutics), heuretics adds to these critical and interpretive practices a generative productivity of the sort practiced in the avant-garde' (Ulmer 1994a: xii).

6 While the term *écriture* is quite simply a translation of the French word for 'writing,' it has come to be associated in critical theory with the playful, deconstruc-

tive language of the poststructuralists. This allows for a convenient pun on the abbreviation for Electronic Critique, which is 'e-crit.'

7 For a more detailed reading of how Kittler serves as an appropriate exemplar for students of digital media, see my articles 'You Can't Always Get What You Want: Transparency and Deception on the Computer Fashion Scene' (*Ctheory*, December 2000) and 'Friedrich Kittler's Media Scenes: An Instruction Manual' (*Postmodern Culture* 10.1 [Oct. 1999]).

8 Gregory Ulmer, who coined the term 'electracy,' explains it in the following manner: 'In the history of human culture there are but three apparatuses: orality, literacy, and now electracy. We live in the moment of the emergence of electracy, comparable to the two principal moments of literacy (The Greece of Plato, and the Europe of Galileo)' (http://www.elf.ufl.edu/electracy.html).

9 In this study, I use the term 'picture theory' in the same punning sense as Mitchell. Picture theory is both about the theories of pictures and also about picturing theory – that is, making pictures more of a staple in critical theory, and inventing methods that incorporate pictures as part of theoretical discourse.

10 The method that I am proposing here would go beyond those of Hayles and McLuhan, which involve the coupling of a designer to a writer, as if the graphicness of the text were an afterthought or a gimmick. The graphic elements of Hayles's text do succeed in pointing to the materiality of her subjects of investigation, but my goal is to have the graphicness drive the production of the text itself. I am attempting to invent a mode of discourse in which the images themselves are theories, and not merely reminders of the materiality of discourse.

11 Note that the word 'node,' which is now the commonplace term for a single HTML document within a hypertext (i.e., 'hypertext node'), is also the term used by Freud to describe the process of condensation. In a dream, various associations can intersect in a single ideational node. See Freud 1976: 383ff.

12 The most obvious 'celebration of ocular madness' in the texts considered here is that of Rosalind Krauss, *The Political Unconscious*, a study of avant-garde optics. Traces of this 'madness' might also be observed in the texts of Ulmer and Ray, due mainly to the fact that they draw heavily on the avant-garde arts in their work. It would be wrong, however, to consider any of these texts as a mere 'celebration,' for they all view the avant-garde as a means to an end. Like Breton, in the *Surrealist Manifesto*, each of these critics might explore the possibilities of ocular madness in one form or another, but only to 'submit them, should the occasion arise, to the control of reason' (Breton 1991: 66). It is the firm intention of this study to pursue the same rules of the game.

13 There is an obvious resonance here with psychoanalytic theory, particularly dream analysis, the goal of which is for the analyst to determine the analysand's repressed 'mental set.' Gombrich, of course, is quite aware of this resonance: 'In psychology this process is more frequently labelled "projection." We say we "project" the familiar images into vaguely similar shapes of clouds. It is well known that this propensity of our minds is used in modern psychiatry as a diag-

nostic tool. In the so-called "Rorschach test," standard inkblots are offered to the subject for interpretation' (1969: 105).

14 The terms 'imagetext' and 'image/text' are taken directly from W.J.T. Mitchell's picture theory. 'Imagetext' is simply used to designate 'composite, synthetic works (or concepts) that combine image and text' (1994: 89n). Mitchell employs the slash to identify 'image/text' as 'a problematic gap, cleavage, or rupture in representation' (89n).

15 Studies of visuality which cite Plato's anti-pictorialism are legion. For an exemplary selection, see Gombrich's extended commentary on Plato's view of the 'unreliability' of the image (1969: 126).

16 The New Critical drive to redefine 'literature' and the canon is studied in great depth by John Guillory. See especially chapter 3 of *Cultural Capital*, 'Ideology and Canonical Form: The New Critical Canon.'

17 In the words of Gregory Ulmer, '... the issue is less how art criticism can best serve art than how art can serve as a fruitful realm for critical and theoretical activity' (1994b: 81).

18 See Jean-Claude Lebensztejn's 'Starting Out from the Frame: Vignettes' for an account of how the avant-garde challenged the boundary between art and reality by 'interfering with the frame' of art (130).

19 For a detailed analysis of surrealist methodology, and its application to current critical and pedagogical methodologies, see Robert Ray, *The Avant-Garde Finds Andy Hardy* and Gregory Ulmer, *Heuretics*.

20 In 'Modernizing Vision,' Jonathan Crary identifies the *mise en abyme* as an important device of the baroque, and its practitioners include William Blake, who emerges in the next chapter. The *mise en abyme* is also evident in the work of Ulmer, who sees it as a 'formal device for simulating intuition' (1994a: 145). See Ulmer 1983 for a more detailed account of the place of the baroque in deconstruction.

21 The place of mnemonics in digital-centric discourse is discussed briefly in chapter 3. For a more detailed summary of the place of mnemonics, or 'secondary mnemonics,' in the electronic age, see Ulmer 1994a: especially 191ff. One goal of a new 'hyperrhetoric' might be to reintegrate the art of mnemonics into everyday discourse, thereby intervening in the computer-centric mania for liquidating all memory into the ether of electrons.

22 Nelson Hilton tackles this question in 'Golgonooza Text,' a Flash-based piece that allows for animated comparisons of plates in *The Book of Urizen* and *The Four Zoas*. As Hilton indicates, 'This piece includes some incidental reflections on the curiosity of public domain text and copyright image, the organization of the Blake Archive, and the need for the ability to deep-link to its resources' (http://www.rc.umd.edu/praxis/designsonblake/abstracts.html#hilton).

3. The Hypericonic De-Vise

1 In a detailed and complex image that has been called Ramus's 'Allegory of the Tree,' the great logician portrays himself as a tree, complete with 'branching

dichotomies,' which is threatened by, but ultimately more powerful than, Aristotelian logic. See Ong 1958: 208 for a detailed description of this allegory and its relevance to the Ramus/Aristotle conflict.

2 In a prefatory message to the reader of *The Underwood* (1640–1), Jonson writes: 'With the same leave, the ancients called that kind of body *sylva* ... in which there were works of diverse nature and matter congested, as the multitude call timbertrees, promiscuously growing, a wood or forest; so am I bold to entitle these lesser poems of later growth by this of *Underwood*, out of the analogy they hold to *The Forest* in my former book, and no otherwise' (Jonson 1985: 307).

3 This division of educational practices falls in line with the Academic (Greek) and Clerical (Western) educational archetypes identified by Carl A. Raschke (2003: 53–5).

4 Geoffrey Summerfield offers the following synopsis of *An Island in the Moon*: 'Mechanistic notions of consciousness, a utilitarian view of what was worth knowing, a fashion for moralizing cant, the spread of an infantine proto-science, a largely prudential moral orthodoxy, the enthusiasm of the Man of Feeling, the encyclopaedic aspirations of dutiful children – all are poured into Blake's topsy-turvy lunar world, and given a good shaking' (1985: 214).

5 For a more extensive attempt to unravel the meaning of Blake's 'Fourfold Vision,' see McGann 1973.

6 Readers with a genealogical penchant may want to consider Newton, here, as a link in an epistemological chain whose primary role was to devise a logical organization of space. Other links in the chain, according to Ong, include the 'Copernican way of thinking about space which would lead to Newtonian physics, ... the evolution of the painter's vision climaxed by Jan van Eyck's use of the picture frame as diaphragm ... the topical logics of Rudolph Agricola and Ramus, as well as ... other phenomena' (1958: 83). The enigmatic presence of Newton in Blake's work has him appearing most often as a figure constrained by the bounds of reason. This subject is examined by Donald Ault in *Visionary Physics: Blake's Response to Newton*. See also W.J.T. Mitchell's essay 'Chaosthetics: Blake's Sense of Form,' in which the author contrasts Newton's 'hyperorganized world' to Blake's world of chaos (180).

7 The potential, here, for a Marxist reading of Blake's attitude toward commercial engraving is undeniable. Eaves comes closest to such a reading, producing two anti-bourgeois 'artificial myths': 'The Counter-Arts Conspiracy,' which confronts capitalist machinations in the art world, and 'The Age of Blake,' a historical invention which challenges the hegemonic, bourgeois construction of the Romantic canon.

8 The most zealous advocate of education as imitation in Blake's day was perhaps Sir Joshua Reynolds, who lectured regularly at the Academy and whom Blake ridiculed on several accounts, filling the margins of Reynolds's *Discourses* with vituperative annotations. In one of his lectures to the Academy, Reynolds insisted that 'students should not presume to think themselves qualified to invent, till they were acquainted with those stores of invention the world already possesses,

and had by that means accumulated sufficient materials for the mind to work with' (1959: 222).

9 The following passage from Viscomi is indicative of the extent to which the 'infernal method' allegory might be pursued:

> The bite [of the acid] would have been very active, given the amount of metal exposed, but if it grew too active it would have become cloudy and emitted nitric oxide, 'which in Hell' may be 'salutary and medicinal,' but on earth is harmful. Blake may be alluding to such fiery biting when he asserts that 'melting apparent surfaces away, and displaying the infinite which was hid' characterized 'printing in the infernal method.' (1993: 81)

10 At this point, hypericonomy draws me into a myriad successive readings of this imagetext, which would strengthen this study if it were conducted in a hypertext environment. Among the discursive circuits that run through this outlet, we might consider the following: the role of the nurse, as opposed to the father or mother, in educating a child; the role that the seated child plays in this picture, especially considering the fact that she is engaging in a bookish activity, and that she too is 'enframed' (this time, by a doorway); the mingling of the baroque-looking vines with the actual letters of the poem, a detail which is especially significant to a study guided by the vise image (etymology of 'vise' = *vitis*, Latin for vine, only later associated with the screw of the vise). The network of scholarly trajectories (i.e., domestic history, pedagogic history, iconology, etymology, etc.) which pass through the node of Blake's 'Nurse's Song' cannot be covered adequately in an essay of this scope; nor would this web of concatenations be appropriately represented in a medium which must limit itself to a couple hundred printed sheets of paper. I would argue, however, that such a multifaceted, multidisciplinary undertaking would be appropriate to an electronic medium that supports the gathering of various discourses provided by a collaborative effort at a single ideational node. Hypericonomy calls for this multidisciplinary collaboration and its crossing with the subjective discursive elements of each collaborator – without relegating any of these discursive circuits to the confines of a footnote.

11 Richard Coyne draws on the term 'technoromanticism' to identify narratives that promote an emancipatory vision of new technologies. In Coyne's words, 'It is easy to show how romanticism encourages inflated expectations, diminishes tangible concerns with equipment and embodiment, promotes the heroism of the digital entrepreneur, and dresses conservative thinking in the guise of radicalism' (2001: ix). Although it is beyond the scope of this study, it is tempting to think how Coyne's definition of 'technoromanticism' might be altered if Coyne had supplemented his understanding of Romanticism with the art, philosophy, and technics of William Blake. Of course, Blake is not a 'typical' Romantic, which makes him especially useful in this study, which seeks to disrupt compartmentalization, specialization, and even common stereotyping, as exemplified, for example, in the pervasive, simplistic use of the term 'Romantic.'

4. Nonsense and Play

1 See playdium.com for additional details. Readers who followed the hypericonic motif of the last chapter will find it ironic (or perhaps appropriate?) that the flash interface used at the Playdium site (as of 9.20.03) features a vise-like apparatus which enframes video clips of children playing simulation games.

2 This figure is borrowed from Neisser 2003; it is based on a model by P.A. Carpenter, M.A. Just, and P. Shell which appeared in an article entitled 'What One Intelligence Test Measures: A Theoretical Account of the Processing in the Raven Progressive Matrices Test' (*Psychological Review* 97 [1990]: 404–31). Neisser explains the test as follows: 'It [the test] requires visual analysis as well as the ability to keep track of a hierarchy of operations and goals ... The pattern on top is missing a piece, and a test-taker must determine which of the numbered pieces below will complete it' (ncap3.html).

3 The concept that cognitive skills can be media specific might be considered alongside McLuhan's conception of the media's impact on sense ratios: '... the effect of the entry of the TV image will vary from culture to culture in accordance with the existing sense ratios in each culture. In audile-tactile Europe TV has intensified the visual sense, spurring them toward American styles of packaging and dressing. In America, the intensely visual culture, TV has opened the doors of audile-tactile perception to the nonvisual world of spoken languages and food and the plastic arts' (McLuhan 1994: 45). McLuhan's choice of William Blake's *Jerusalem* to elucidate this concept (46) should not be surprising in the context of this study.

4 In *What Video Games Have to Teach Us about Learning and Literacy* (Palgrave, 2003), James Paul Gee makes a similar argument, suggesting that we look to well-designed video games for cues in the development of more effective teaching methodologies.

5 The term 'delirium' is used deliberately here, based on the etymology in which the word is rooted: in Latin, *de* + *lirare*, which means, literally, to 'go out of the furrow.' The importance of 'going out of the furrow' shall return in the final chapter. In the *Manifeste du surréalisme* (1924), Breton betrays the surrealist longing for childhood in the following delirious passage, among others: 'S'il [l'homme] garde sa lucidité, il ne peut que se retourner alors vers son enfance qui, pour massacrée qu'elle ait été par le soin des dresseurs, ne lui en semble pas moins pleine de charmes. Là, l'absence de toute rigueur connue lui laisse la perspective de plusieurs vies menées à la fois; il s'enracine dans cette illusion; il ne veut plus connaître que la facilité momentanée, extrême, de toutes choses. Chaque matin, des enfants partent sans inquiétude. Tout est près, les pires conditions matérielles sont excellentes. Les bois sont blancs ou noirs, on ne dormira jamais' (14).

6 See Mitchell's *Iconology* for a depiction of the *camera obscura* as a Marxian 'hyper-icon' which embodies the concept of ideology: '... as Marx would say, the image behind the concept [of ideology], is the *camera obscura*, literally a "dark room" or

box in which images are projected. The image behind the concept of commodity, on the other hand, is the fetish or idol, an object of superstition' (162).

7 'Je crois à la résolution future de ces deux états, en apparence si contradictoires, que sont le rêve et la réalité, en une sorte de réalité absolue, de surréalité, si l'on peut ainsi dire' (Breton 1991: 24).

8 Q: What do you get when you cross an orange? A: Peanut butter, elephants can't swim!!!
    Q: Is it faster to Chicago or by bus? A: Yes, but where do I send the fish?
    Q: What's the difference between a typewriter? A: Half a zipper.
    Q: What's the difference between a dead bird? A: His other leg is just as long!
    (copied from an e-mail joke list archived at www.frogtown.com).

9 See *A Book of Surrealist Games*, by Alastair Brotchie and Mel Gooding (Boston: Shambhala, 1995), for a wide selection of examples demonstrating the surrealists' attempts to experience and document a childlike mental state. This highly entertaining and sometimes shocking text describes a variety of methods for achieving a child's frame of mind, including a vast collection of instructions for games and art projects gleaned from the archives of childhood pastimes.

10 It seems appropriate, here, to invoke Derrida's problematization of the notion of 'frame' or *'parergon'* in *The Truth in Painting*: 'I do not know what is essential and what is accessory in a work,' Derrida writes. 'And above all I do not know what this thing is, that is neither essential nor accessory, neither proper nor improper, and that Kant calls *parergon*, for example the frame. Where does the frame take place. Does it take place. Where does it begin. Where does it end. What is its internal limit. Its external limit. And its surface between the two limits' (63). *The Truth in Painting* undertakes a deconstruction of the figure/ground binary, a dialectical construction which Derrida undermines by means of the *trait* and its emblem, the *passe-partout*. It might also be appropriate to consider, here, Heidegger's conception of enframing (*gestell*) as the essence of technology (see 'The Question concerning Technology'), and the way in which nonsense thwarts the technological drive toward efficiency. I shall leave that discussion to another project.

11 I use the term 'remainder' here as a direct reference to Jean-Jacques Lecercle's essential study of nonsense, *The Violence of Language*. This concept is dealt with explicitly in the first chapter.

12 In an essay entitled, 'Where's Poppa? or, The Defeminization of Blake's "Little Black Boy,"' Donald Ault provides an ideographic reading of the poem, suggesting that 'being black is parallel to being born, but punctuation that visually suggests gender difference (the vaginal "O" and the phallic "!") interrupts that continuity and implies that (at this point) white ... is not what he [the Little Black Boy] wishes he were but rather an intrusion into his identity, a contamination of his pure "black" ... identity (his "I," associated with his mother)' (1990: 78). This reading complexifies our understanding of the poem and undermines a reading which complacently views the Little Black Boy as content with his lot. The poem is further complexified by the fact that Blake only sometimes depicts a black boy on the second plate of the poem, in which two children are accompanied by a Christ-like fig-

ure. A number of critics have investigated the semiotic variability created by Blake's inconsistent designs – for a deconstructive approach, see Carr 1986.

13 At this point, the track of hypericonomy crosses, perhaps catastrophically, with the track of Abraham and Torok's *cryptonomy*, as introduced in *The Wolf Man's Magic Word*. Cryptonomy describes both a psychic reflex of introjection involving puns and macaronics, and the psychoanalytic methodology employed to decipher this introjection. Evidence of the similarity of the two methodologies may be observed in Derrida's description of cryptonomy as 'a return of the childhood knowledge of English, a (conscious-unconscious) translation machine almost perfect in its finality' (1986: xxxvii). Hypericonomy does indeed share many qualities with, and even borrows from, cryptonomy. But the crucial difference is that hypericonomy is more concerned with cultural and scholarly problems than with treating psychic neuroses. Of course, if the hypericonic 'tuning knobs' were adjusted appropriately, hypericonomy might very well become a psychotherapeutic device.

14 In *The Avant-Garde Finds Andy Hardy*, Robert Ray describes the frontispieces of Hardy Boys books as 'an oasis, something to look forward to while trekking through the terrifyingly unillustrated pages: it sustained hope, and like a magnet, pulled readers through what might otherwise have been put aside' (124).

15 I would like to believe that hypericonomy places its creator in 'the right place' for the experience of the sublime. That place is identified by Derrida as a paradoxical place:

> Whence this apparently paradoxical conclusion: the right place, the ideal *topos* for the experience of the sublime, for the inadequation of presentation to the unpresentable, will be a median place, an average place of the body which would provide an aesthetic maximum without losing itself in the mathematical infinite. Things must come to a relationship of body to body: the 'sublime' body (the one that provokes the feeling of the sublime) must be far enough away for the maximum size to appear and remain sensible, but close enough to be seen and 'comprehended,' not to lose itself in the mathematical indefinite. Regulated, measured distance [*é-loignement*] *between* a too-close and a too-far. (1987: 130)

5. From Écriture to E-Crit

1 While Guillory focuses here on humanities education as an empty form of cultural remediation, I have attempted to focus on how the humanities might play a key role in remediating (in the sense of both Guillory and Jay Bolter and Richard Grusin) higher education.

2 Manovich discusses this theory at length in 'Avant-Garde as Software' (http://www.manovich.net/docs/avantgarde_as_software.doc; accessed October 2003).

3 This self-accusation, in earnest, was partly motivated by the accusation of my anti-nostalgic colleague Nick Rombes, who is a co-founder of the E-Crit Program.

Works Cited

Abraham, Nicolas, and Maria Torok. 1986. *The Wolf Man's Magic Word: A 'Crypton-omy.'* Trans. Nicholas Rand. Minneapolis: University of Minnesota Press.

Agricola, Rudolph. 1958. *De Inventione Dialectica* (1479). In *Ramus, Method, and the Decay of Dialogue: From the Art of Discourse to the Art of Reason*, by Walter J. Ong. Cambridge: Harvard University Press.

Argan, Giulio. 1980. 'Ideology and Iconology.' In *The Language of Images*, ed. W.J.T. Mitchell. Chicago: University of Chicago Press.

Arseth, Espen. 1997. *Cybertext: Perspectives on Ergodic Literature*. Baltimore: Johns Hopkins University Press.

Ault, Donald. 1974. *Visionary Physics: Blake's Response to Newton*. Chicago: University of Chicago Press.

– 1990. 'Where's Poppa: Or the Defeminization of Blake's "Little Black Boy."' In *Out of Bounds: Male Writers and Gender(ed) Criticism*, ed. Laura Claridge and Elizabeth Langland. Amherst: University of Massachusetts Press.

Barbauld, Anna Laetitia. 1781. *Hymns in Prose for Children*. London: J. Johnson.

Barnes, Julian. 1989. *A History of the World in 10½ Chapters*. New York: Vintage.

Barthes, Roland. 1974. *S/Z: An Essay*. Trans. Richard Miller. New York: Hill and Wang.

– 1977. *Image, Music, Text*. Trans. Stephen Heath. New York: Hill and Wang.

– 1992. *Mythologies*. Trans. Annette Lavers. New York: Noonday.

Benjamin, Walter. 1989. 'N [Re the Theory of Knowledge, Theory of Progress].' Trans. Leigh Hafrey and Richard Sieburth. In *Benjamin – Philosophy, Aesthetics, History*, ed. Gary Smith et al. Chicago: University of Chicago Press.

Blake, William. 1988. *The Complete Poetry and Prose of William Blake*. Ed. David V. Erdman. New York: Doubleday.

Bolter, Jay David. 1991. *Writing Space: Hypertext, Literary Theory and the History of the Book*. Cambridge: Cambridge University Press.

Bolter, Jay David, and Richard Grusin. 2000. *Remediation: Understanding New Media*. Cambridge: MIT Press.

Breton, André. 1991. 'Manifeste du surréalisme (1924).' In *Manifestes du surréalisme*. Paris: Folio.

Brunette, Peter, and David Wills. 1994. 'The Spatial Arts: An Interview with Jacques Derrida.' In *Deconstruction and the Visual Arts*, ed. Peter Brunette and David Wills. Cambridge: Cambridge University Press.

Carpenter, P.A., M.A. Just, and P. Shell. 1990. 'What One Intelligence Test Measures: A Theoretical Account of the Processing in the Raven Progressive Matrices Test.' *Psychological Review* 97: 404–31.

Carr, Stephen Leo. 1986. 'Illuminated Printing: Toward a Logic of Difference.' In *Unnam'd Forms: Blake and Textuality*. Berkeley: University of California Press.

Carroll, Lewis. 1963. *The Annotated Alice: 'Alice's Adventures in Wonderland' and 'Through the Looking Glass.'* Ed. Martin Gardner. New York: World Publishing Company.

Carson, Shelly H., Jordan B. Peterson, and Daniel M. Higgin. 2003. 'Decreased Latent Inhibition Is Associated with Increased Creative Achievement in High- Functioning Individuals.' *Journal of Personality and Social Psychology* 85.3 (Sept.): 499–506.

Cooper, Andrew, and Michael Simpson. 1999. 'The High-Tech Luddite of Lambeth: Blake's Eternal Hacking.' *Wordsworth Circle* 30.3 (Summer): 125–31.

Coyne, Richard. 2001. *Technoromanticism*. Cambridge: MIT Press.

Crary, Jonathan. 1988. 'Modernizing Vision.' In *Vision and Visuality*, ed. Hal Foster. Dia Art Foundation Discussions in Contemporary Culture, no. 2. Seattle: Bay Press.

Deleuze, Gilles. 1969. *The Logic of Sense*. Trans. Mark Lester. New York: Columbia University Press.

– 1986. *Foucault*. Minneapolis: University of Minnesota Press.

Deleuze, Gilles, and Felix Guattari. *Anti-Oedipus: Capitalism and Schizophrenia*. 1983. Trans. Robert Hurley, Mark Seem, and Helen R. Lane. Minneapolis: University of Minnesota Press.

– 1987. *A Thousand Plateaus: Capitalism and Schizophrenia*. Minneapolis: University of Minnesota Press.

Derrida, Jacques. 1984. *Of Grammatology*. Baltimore: Johns Hopkins University Press.

– 1986. 'Fors: The Anglish Words of Nicolas Abraham and Maria Torok.' In *The Wolf Man's Magic Word: A 'Cryptonomy,'* by Nicolas Abraham and Maria Torok. Trans. Nicholas Rand. Theory and History of Literature, vol. 37. Minneapolis: University of Minnesota Press.

– 1987. *The Truth in Painting*. Chicago: University of Chicago Press.

– 1996. *Archive Fever: A Freudian Impression*. Trans. Eric Prenowitz. Chicago: University of Chicago Press.

Drucker, Johanna 1994. *The Visible Word: Experimental Typography and Modern Art, 1909–1923*. Chicago: University of Chicago Press.

Eagleton, Terry. 2003. *After Theory*. New York: Basic Books.

Eaves, Morris. 1992. *The Counter-Arts Conspiracy: Art and Industry in the Age of Blake*. Ithaca: Cornell University Press.

Erdman, David V., ed. 1988. *The Complete Poetry and Prose of William Blake*. Newly Revised Edition. New York: Doubleday.

Feyerabend, Paul. 1975. *Against Method*. London: New Left Books.

Foucault, Michel. 1971. *The Archaeology of Knowledge and the Discourse on Language*. Trans. A.M. Sheridan Smith. New York: Pantheon.

– 1982. *This Is Not a Pipe*. Trans. James Harkness. Berkeley and Los Angeles: University of California Press.

– 1994. *The Order of Things: An Archaeology of the Human Sciences*. New York: Vintage.

Freud, Sigmund. 1976. *The Interpretation of Dreams*. Ed. Angela Richards. Trans. James Strachey. London: Penguin Books.

Frow, John. 1986. *Marxism and Literary History*. Oxford: Basil Blackwell.

Gehl, John. 1996. 'The Curriculum Has Run Its Course.' *Educom Review* 31.6. http://www.educause.edu/pub/er/review/reviewArticles/31604.html (accessed 18 April 2005).

Gitelman, Lisa, and Geoffrey Pingree. 2003. *New Media, 1740–1915*. Cambridge: MIT Press.

Gleber, Conrad. 2004. 'Editor's Note.' *International Digital Media and Arts Association Journal* 1.1 (Spring): 1–2.

Goethe, Johann Wolfgang von. 1990. *Faust*. Trans. Walter Kaufmann. New York: Doubleday.

Gombrich, E.H. 1969. *Art and Illusion: A Study in the Psychology of Pictorial Representation*. Princeton: Princeton University Press.

Griffin, Matthew. 1996. 'Technologies of Writing: Interview with Friedrich A. Kittler.' *New Literary History* 27.4 (Autumn): 731–42.

Guillory, John. 1993. *Cultural Capital: The Problem of Literary Canon Formation*. Chicago: University of Chicago Press.

Harvey, David. 1989. *The Condition of Postmodernity: An Enquiry into the Origins of Cultural Change*. Oxford and New York: Blackwell.

Hayles, Katherine. 2002. *Writing Machines*. Cambridge: MIT Press.

Heidegger, Martin. 1977. *The Question Concerning Technology and Other Essays*. Trans. William Lovitt. New York: Harper and Row.

Hilton, Nelson. 2005. 'Golgonooza Text.' Romantic Circles Praxis Series. http://www.rc.umd.edu/praxis/designsonblake/hilton/hilton.html (accessed 18 April 2005).

Hughes, Robert. 1996. *The Shock of the New*. New York: Alfred A. Knopf.

Jay, Martin. 1988. 'Scopic Regimes of Modernity.' In *Vision and Visuality*, ed. Hal Foster. Dia Art Foundation Discussions in Contemporary Culture, no. 2. Seattle: Bay Press.

Jonson, Ben. 1985. *The Oxford Authors: Ben Jonson*. Ed. Ian Donaldson. Oxford and New York: Oxford University Press.

Jung, Carl G. 1964. *Man and His Symbols*. New York: Doubleday.

Kittler, Friedrich A. 1990. *Discourse Networks, 1800/1900*. Trans. Michael Metter with Chris Cullens. Stanford: Stanford University Press.

Krauss, Rosalind E. 1994. *The Optical Unconscious*. Cambridge: MIT Press.

Lacan, Jacques. 1977. *Le séminaire, livre XX: Encore*. Paris: Seuil.

Lanham, Richard. 1993. *The Electronic Word: Democracy, Technology, and the Arts.* Chicago: University of Chicago Press.

Leader, Zachary. 1981. *Reading Blake's Songs.* London: Routledge & Kegan Paul.

Lebensztejn, Jean-Claude. 1994. 'Starting Out from the Frame: Vignettes.' In *Deconstruction and the Visual Arts*, ed. Peter Brunette and David Wills. Cambridge: Cambridge University Press.

Lecercle, Jean-Jacques. 1990. *The Violence of Language.* London and New York: Routledge.

Lévi-Strauss, Claude. 1967. *Structural Anthropology.* New York: Doubleday.

– 1970. *The Raw and the Cooked.* New York: Harper and Row.

Lewis, Virginia L. 1992. 'A German Poststructuralist.' *PLL* 28.1 (Winter): 100–6.

Liu, Alan. 2005. 'Philosophy of This Site: Perspectives on the Romantic Chronology by Its Editors.' The Romantic Chronology. http://english.ucsb.edu:591/rchrono/philosophy.htm (accessed 19 April 2005).

Lynch, Jack. 1997. 'Hideous Progeny, Version 0.4 Beta.' http://www.english.upenn.edu/~jlynch/Frank/mla.html (Nov.).

Manovich, Lev. 2000. *The Language of New Media.* Cambridge: MIT Press.

McGann, Jerome. 1973. 'The Aim of Blake's Prophecies and the Uses of Blake Criticism.' In *Blake's Sublime Allegory*, ed. Stuart Curran and Joseph Anthony Wittreich, Jr. Madison: University of Wisconsin Press.

– 1991. 'How to Read a Book.' In *The Textual Condition.* Princeton: Princeton University Press.

McLuhan, Marshall. 1994. *Understanding Media.* Cambridge: MIT Press.

Mitchell, W.J.T. 1978. *Blake's Composite Art.* Princeton: Princeton University Press.

– 1986. *Iconology: Image, Text, Ideology.* Chicago: University of Chicago Press.

– 1994. *Picture Theory.* Chicago: University of Chicago Press.

– 1997. 'Chaosthetics: Blake's Sense of Form.' In *William Blake: Images and Texts.* San Marino, CA: Huntington Library.

Murner, Thomas. 1958. *Chartiludium logice* (*Logical Card Game*) (1509). In *Ramus, Method, and the Decay of Dialogue: From the Art of Discourse to the Art of Reason*, by Walter J. Ong. Cambridge: Harvard University Press.

Neisser, Ulric. 2003. 'Rising Scores on Intelligence Tests.' *American Scientist* 85 (Sept.–Oct.): 440–7. http://www.americanscientist.org/template/AssetDetail/assetid/24612?fulltext=true (accessed 23 Oct. 2003).

Novak, Marcos. 1992. 'Liquid Architectures in Cyberspace.' In *Cyberspace: First Steps*, ed. Michael Benedikt. Cambridge: MIT Press.

O'Gorman, Marcel. 1\0. 1998. http://web.nwe.ufl.edu/~ogorman/Blake/10intro.html (June).

– 2001. 'A Fever for Archiving: How Humanities Scholarship Works the Web.' *Space and Culture* 10 (Spring): 31–46.

Ong, Walter J. 1958. *Ramus, Method, and the Decay of Dialogue: From the Art of Discourse to the Art of Reason.* Cambridge: Harvard University Press.

Panofsky, Erwin. 1962. *Studies in Iconology.* New York: Harper & Row.

Pope John XXI (Peter of Spain). 1945. *Summulae logicales*. Trans. Joseph P. Mullally. In *The Summulae logicales of Peter of Spain*. Notre Dame, Indiana.

Postman, Neil. 1986. *Amusing Ourselves to Death*. New York: Penguin Books.

Prenowitz, Eric. 1996. *'Right on [à même]' Archive Fever*. Chicago: University of Chicago Press.

Ramus, Peter. 1958a. *Dialecticae institutiones* (1543). In *Ramus, Method, and the Decay of Dialogue: From the Art of Discourse to the Art of Reason*, by Walter J. Ong. Cambridge: Harvard University Press.

– 1958b. *Three Commentaries on Dialectic Published under the Authorship of Omer Talon* (1546). In *Ramus, Method, and the Decay of Dialogue: From the Art of Discourse to the Art of Reason*, by Walter J. Ong. Cambridge: Harvard University Press.

Raschke, Carl A. 2003. *The Digital Revolution and the Coming of the Postmodern University*. New York: RoutledgeFalmer.

Ray, Robert. 1995. *The Avant-Garde Finds Andy Hardy*. Cambridge: Harvard University Press.

Read, Dennis M. 1981. 'The Context of Blake's "Public Address": Cromek and the Chalcographic Society.' *Philological Quarterly* 60: 69–86.

Reynolds, Sir Joshua. 1959. *Discourses on Art*. Ed. Robert R. Wark. San Marino, CA: Huntington Library.

Rousseau, Jean-Jacques. 1762–3. *Émile, ou de l'Éducation*. 4 vols. Amsterdam: Jean Néaulme, 1762. Translated by William Kendrick as *Emilius and Sophia; or, A New System of Education*. 4 vols. London: R. Griffiths, T. Becket & P.A. de Hondt.

Saco, Diana. 2002. *Cybering Democracy: Public Space and the Internet*. Minneapolis: University of Minnesota Press.

Scorsese, Martin, dir. 1995. *Casino*. With Robert DeNiro, Joe Pesce, Sharon Stone, and Alan King. Universal Pictures.

Sebastian, Thomas. 1990. 'Technology Romanticized: Friedrich Kittler's *Discourse Networks 1800/1900*.' Trans. Judith Geerke and Tim Walters. *MLN* 5.3 (April): 583–95.

Sperber, Dan, and Deidre Wilson. 1986. *Relevance: Communication and Cognition*. Cambridge: Harvard University Press.

Spivak, Gayatri. 1976. 'Translator's Preface.' In *Of Grammatology*, by Jacques Derrida. Baltimore: Johns Hopkins University Press.

Stewart, Susan. 1978. *Nonsense: Aspects of Intertextuality in Folklore and Literature*. Baltimore: Johns Hopkins University Press.

Summerfield, Geoffrey. 1985. *Fantasy and Reason: Children's Literature in the Eighteenth Century*. Athens: University of Georgia Press.

Tisdall, Caroline. 1979. *Joseph Beuys*. Catalogue for Guggenheim exhibit. New York.

Türk, Karl Wilhelm Christian Ritter von. 1806. *Beitrage zur Kenntniss einiger deutscher Elementar-Schulanstalten, namentlich der zu Dessau, Leipzig, Heidelberg, Frankfurt am Mayn und Berlin*. Leipzig. Translated by Friedrich Kittler in *Discourse Networks, 1800/1900*.

Ulmer, Gregory. 1983. 'Op Writing: Derrida's Solicitation of Theoria.' In *Displacement: Derrida and After*, ed. Mark Krupnick. Bloomington: Indiana University Press.

– 1984. *Applied Grammatology.* Baltimore: Johns Hopkins University Press.
– 1989. *Teletheory: Grammatology in the Age of Video.* New York: Routledge.
– 1994a. *Heuretics: The Logic of Invention.* Baltimore: Johns Hopkins University Press.
– 1994b. 'The Heuretics of Deconstruction.' In *Deconstruction and the Visual Arts*, ed. Peter Brunette and David Wills. Cambridge: Cambridge University Press.
Viscomi, Joseph. 1993. *Blake and the Idea of the Book.* Princeton: Princeton University Press.
Wellbery, David. 1990. 'Foreword.' In *Discourse Networks, 1800/1900*, by Friedrich Kittler. Stanford: Stanford University Press.
Wilson, Thomas. 1958. *The Rule of Reason* (1553). In *Ramus, Method, and the Decay of Dialogue: From the Art of Discourse to the Art of Reason*, by Walter J. Ong. Cambridge: Harvard University Press.

ILLUSTRATION CREDITS

Bibliothèque Nationale Universitaire, Strasbourg: 3.2

Carpenter, Just, and Shell 1990: 4.2 (adapted with permission)

CNAC/MNAM/Dist. Réunion des Musées Nationaux / Art Resource, NY: 4.3 (© 2005 Artists Rights Society [ARS], New York / ADAGP, Paris)

Fogg Art Museum, Harvard University: 3.5 (© President and Fellows of Harvard College)

Stephen Gibb: 1.2; 2.1; 3.7

Hirshhorn Museum and Sculpture Garden: 2.4 (gift of Joseph H. Hirshhorn, 1966; photograph by Lee Stalsworth)

Estate of Roy Lichtenstein: 4.4

Jack Lynch: 1.1

W.J.T. Mitchell: 5.1 ('William Blake's Pictorial Schemata,' University of Chicago Press, 1978)

Ellis Nadler: 4.5

Marcel O'Gorman: 4.1; 4.6 (http://www.e-crit.net/blake/10/10.html); 4.8 (http://www.e-crit.net/blake/10/light.html)

Photothèque R. Magritte-ADAGP / Art Resource, NY: 2.2 (© 2005 C. Herscovici / Artists Rights Society [ARS], New York)

Lessing J. Rosenwald Collection, The Library of Congress Rare Books and Special Collections Division: 3.4; 3.6; 4.7

Tate Gallery, London / Art Resource, NY: 2.3; 2.5 (© 2005 Frank Stella / Artists Rights Society [ARS], New York)

University of Chicago Press: 3.3

University of Toronto Press: 3.1

INDEX